There's a Green Plastic Monkey in My Purse

AND OTHER WAYS MOTHERHOOD CHANGES US

Jessie Clemence

DISCOVERY HOUSE

PUBLISHERS®

There's a Green Plastic Monkey in My Purse: And Other Ways Motherhood Changes Us

Discovery House is affiliated with RBC Ministries, Grand Rapids, Michigan.

Requests for permission to quote from this book should be directed to: Permissions Department, Discovery House Publishers, P.O. Box 3566, Grand Rapids, MI 49501, or contact us by e-mail at permissionsdept@dhp.org

Scriptures taken from the Holy Bible, New International Version®, NIV®. Copyright © 1973, 1978, 1984 by Biblica, Inc.™ Used by permission of Zondervan. All rights reserved worldwide. www.zondervan.com

Interior design by Michael J. Williams

ISBN: 978-1-57293-747-5

Printed in the United States of America

First printing in 2013

Contents

How Did This Get in Here?

Welcome, my fellow mothers! Have you ever gone through your purse and found something totally unexpected? I did that a while ago, and do you know what I found? If you guessed a green plastic monkey, then you are right! The monkey surprised me because I had forgotten it was in there; it came with my son's drink at a new restaurant. He wanted me to keep it so he couldn't lose it. While I was digging in my purse I also discovered my daughter's sparkly pink lip gloss instead of breath mints. I thought to myself, "When did I become the kind of woman who walks around with green plastic monkeys and Hello Kitty lip gloss in my purse?" The answer, of course, was the moment I gave birth.

Motherhood changes us, doesn't it? But did any of us know *how much* it would change us? I doubt it. I truly doubt it. And frankly, the monkey is the easy part. It's the other changes that have really surprised me. In an effort to acquaint you with the biggest surprises and difficulties I did *not* see coming, here is my life to date:

- Childhood: I was born and raised by a wonderful set of parents. My mother taught me well and I knew I would be a great mother, effortlessly.

- College Years: I graduated with a degree in Family Studies. Whatever information my mother had forgotten to teach me, I now knew.

- Early Career: I worked as a social worker in the foster care system. By combining my informal parenting knowledge with my degree, I was able to keenly spot all the mistakes that the biological and foster parents were making. I stored up many examples of what *not* to do in the coming years.

- First Pregnancy: My pregnancy with Audrey felt like it lasted five years. I realized that gestating wasn't exactly what I expected and grew increasingly nervous about parenting. But I did not panic. I still knew almost everything.

- Early Motherhood: Our daughter quickly rearranged my entire life and I became painfully aware that 1) I did not know anything; 2) motherhood was truckload of work; and 3) I might not survive.

- Temporary Bravery: During a brief respite in Audrey's toddlerhood, things became a little easier. We had adjusted to the workload of parenting, and Audrey learned a whole new set of exciting skills, like walking and talking. I convinced my husband that if we wanted to have another child, we had better do it before I changed my mind.

- The Plot Thickens: Caleb was born, and my experience as a mother became, shall we say, gritty. Although I loved my children with a passion I cannot put into words, most days I was terribly fearful that due to my own exhaustion and lack of abilities I would fail them completely. Despite my misgivings, Audrey thrived and grew into a fabulous little girl while Caleb suffered from emotional problems and tantrums that never changed, no matter how we parented him. Trust me—we tried everything for four years.

- More Recently: Just before Caleb turned five, he was diagnosed with food sensitivities and a new diet stopped most of his tantrums. He began kindergarten and did really well. Things took a happy upswing. We now feel we have enough skills under our belt to parent successfully, at least until our children become teenagers. We've been warned that a whole new set of skills is required for teens.

I don't think I'm alone in my experience. If we're honest, many of us will admit to dreaming up parenting fantasies while we watched diaper commercials. In 99 percent of all such marketing efforts, a happy baby dashes around a sunny room. Her loving parents look on and laugh at her, adoring every bit of her chubby, small self. The house looks tidy and is furnished with new and matching pieces of furniture. The parents look well rested and are dressed in clean khakis and button-down shirts. Of course, we can't smell their house through the TV, but we imagine a home that nice must smell like pot roast, organic green beans, and clean laundry. We turned from the TV and said to our husbands, "I can't wait until we have all of that." Our husbands smiled at us and then returned to their peaceful reading.

Now look around your house right now and tell me if you're on your way to starring in a diaper commercial. Is your house spotless, fashionable, and smelling of pot roast? Are you wearing pressed khakis and a tailored blouse? Have you looked at your baby and felt only love and tenderness every single moment since birth?

If your kids are older, have you recently won a crown for "Best Mother with the Cleanest House and Most Delicious Snacks"? Do you have a minivan that smells of freshly vacuumed carpet and window cleaner? Have you forgotten how to yell, simply because it isn't necessary in your house?

If you can answer yes to any of these questions, this book is not for you. Put it down immediately and write your own book on parenting.

If, however, you feel unqualified to host a diaper commercial in your house and do not expect to win a crown for Best Mother, then this is the book for you. Mothers who need this book have minivans that smell like petrified French fries and pine tree air fresheners. Our wardrobes consist mostly of jeans, flip-flops, and T-shirts with advertisements for the Little League team. We are too frightened of the mess under the bed to actually clean there. We sometimes look at our children and are so angry that we could spit fire out of our mouths. Sometimes this anger is reignited several times a day, for months and years.

Parenting caught us off guard and shoved our harmless fantasies aside. It requires so much more than we anticipated. It derails perfectly innocent plans we made. It demands sacrifices we did not presume to make. It leaves us financially fragile, emotionally spent, and dangerously exhausted.

And yet, with all these sacrifices, we still love our children like mad. We are happy to comfort fears in the middle of the night. We kiss their soft faces while they sleep. We change diapers and fret over rashes. We cry when they climb on that big school bus for the first time, and we trudge to hundreds of wet soccer games to cheer on the sidelines. We patiently explain the same math problem twenty different ways until the light bulb finally goes on.

Our love compels us to act in their best interest. It is (hopefully) what our parents did for us, and what our children will do for their own kids. Yet there is a vast chasm between *wanting* to do what is best for them and *having the ability* to do what is best for them. Let's face it—you can't water a garden with an empty hose. So where do we get the necessary energy and grace?

As a Christian the best advice I get is always from God's Word. When I pray and read the Bible, answers come. Patience is found. Love is revived and anger fades away. I can become the mother I want to be because God is the parent who loved me first. As a mother, I want to be so many things for my kids: patient, peaceful, happy, healthy, pretty, content . . . the list goes on and on. Without God's intervention and provision, I am none of those things. I am a selfish woman who keenly feels each and every sacrifice.

And yet, as I look back over the last ten years, I see something amazing. God has used this time and the trials to develop beautiful things in my heart. I am not the woman

I was. I am more humble, more patient, and more willing to show others grace whether they are my children or not. As I grow into a better mother, I am also growing a stronger relationship with God. I have to believe that God designed the process for just this purpose. God's greatest hope for our lives is that we seek His kingdom and righteousness with all our hearts. Motherhood is certainly expediting that search for me, in no uncertain terms.

God understands our desire to parent our children well. Galatians 4:6–7 says, "Because you are sons, God sent the Spirit of his Son into our hearts, the Spirit who calls out, 'Abba, Father.' So you are no longer a slave, but a son; and since you are a son, God has made you also an heir." Because of God's great love for us and Jesus' sacrifice, we are children of God. *Children of God!* What a beautiful gift.

Joyous benefits come with this status. Our heavenly Father hands us nothing that He doesn't equip us to handle. Think about it—what loving parent would give a child a project and then refuse to help? Refuse to pay for the expenses? Refuse to give instructions or offer wisdom? No, every loving parent does her best to help her children grow and be the best they can be. God does the same for us. We are His children, and He will not leave us to parent alone. He has the money to handle our kids and their growing feet. He knows what our families need and He's ready to provide it, because our children are His children too! He loves them more than we do. He will not fail us if we ask Him for help.

So if you're feeling inadequate for the job of Mother, join the crowd! No one is adequate! We all need to humbly seek God's wisdom and blessings to raise these children. Join me for the following chapters where we'll discuss how to be those patient, peaceful, and content mothers our kids need.

While we gradually nurture these character traits, together we'll grow a deeper relationship with our God.

Study Questions

1. What has been the most surprising joy about being a mother?
2. What has been your biggest disappointment in motherhood?
3. What character trait do you most want to develop for your children's sakes? Why?
4. Please examine 2 Corinthians 5:17–18 and Ephesians 4:22–24. How has parenting helped you become a new person in Christ? How has parenting helped you mature?

IS THIS BOOK FOR YOU?

1. Flip up the cushions of your couch. What do you find?
   a. Twelve tiny cars and a lot of crushed crackers.
   b. My friend Andy's cell phone and twenty dollars in change.
   c. Nothing. I vacuumed there last week, three times. It's still clean.

2. How many pairs of shoes are in your entryway?
   a. Fifty. Five people live here and we each have a pair of flip flops, one pair of church shoes, and sneakers. Plus we have an eight-year-old daughter, so she has ten extra pairs of sparkly ballet slippers and boots with fur. And the neighbor kids are here someplace, so that probably explains those shoes I don't recognize.
   b. Six. Why are you asking?
   c. Ten. My husband and I each have a few, of course, but then I added a couple of adorable booties I found on sale last week. We've lined them up next to our big shoes and it's just *so cute*!

3. Pretend that you are going to put your car up for sale today and examine the car's interior for cleanliness. What do you need to do before a prospective buyer sees it?
   a. I don't know. How do you get melted crayon out of the back window? Can I just set fire to the car and start fresh? Seriously, there isn't a person on earth who could get this car clean enough to sell.
   b. I need to get that coffee mug out of the cup holder, for sure.

c. Well, the car is clean but we already have all the baby stuff strapped in, just in case. So it would take me twenty minutes to get out the car seat, the stroller, and my suitcase for the hospital, and my mom is planted in the backseat refusing to move. She doesn't want to miss anything exciting. I don't know how to get her out.

4. Take the hose attachment from your vacuum and stick it into the dark recess under a large piece of furniture. What happens?

a. I know from experience that I will suck up a tiny doll and/or a bouncy ball, which will clog the vacuum. I will then have to take a knitting needle and start poking around in the hose to pop the toy out. This will take twenty minutes, and I will be covered in dust and very irritated when it's over. Then I will promise to never vacuum under there again. And I am a woman of my word. Don't look under the china cabinet.

b. I will probably suck up that diamond earring I dropped last Friday when my husband and I returned home from dinner and a Broadway show.

c. Oh, we don't have any large pieces of furniture. They aren't safe for babies, so we took them all out or lowered them directly to the floor.

Add up your answers. If your answers were mostly:

As This is the book for you, but you already knew that. I hope I don't insult your intelligence by telling you things you already know. At least you'll never feel like you're alone!

Bs This is not the book for you. I don't know why you're reading it, but maybe you have friends you can help with the stories you read in these pages.

Cs You are totally ready to be a mom and totally cute. You also totally need to read this book to prepare for what you're about to experience. Welcome!

WHAT HAS BEEN THE BIGGEST SHOCK OF MOTHERHOOD?

(I interview my friends. It's one of the hazards they face by being friends with a writer.)

- I've had to learn that it's not all about me. —Jenny, mother of three

- The fatigue factor. I didn't sleep through the night for almost five years. —Melissa, mother of two teens

- When they graduated and left home for college. —Grandma Freda, mother of nine, stepmother to seven

- The ignorance of other people. My husband and I are white and our adopted boys are black. —Melody, mother of two

- How much time I spend thinking about my son, and now his family. An old saying says that having a child is like having your heart walk around outside of your body. So true! —Sandy, mother of one grown son

- The lack of sleep. I love sleep. I used to be able to go to sleep early, sleep late, and count on not waking up at night, ever. —Sara, mother of three

- How fast time goes and how much more laid back I have become. —Shana, mother of four

- The amount of work! —Deb, mother of six

- The depth of feeling I have for my children and how they can affect me so much emotionally. —Barb, mother of four grown children

CHAPTER 1

I Want to Be
a Selfless Mother

In our generation, most of us grew up with an idea that we would have a career *and* a family. We've been taught that we can have it all. And truthfully, some of us can do it all and balance it quite nicely, thank you. For an example, my doctor is somewhere in her mid-thirties, compassionate, and whip-smart. I have yet to experience a medical predicament that she hasn't been able to figure out. Currently the dear woman is on maternity leave because she just had her fourth child. The woman balances a medical career with four children and a house and a husband. And yet she has never once come into the exam room and fallen asleep in her chair. The woman has far more grace and stamina than most of us do, and good for her!

The rest of us may have to make a few sacrifices here and there. I know the plans I had for my life, but reality demanded that I make adjustments to my priorities. I know that I am not alone in these adjustments. Let's take a moment to discuss how motherhood changes our plans and teaches us about God's selfless love for us.

Let's Get Those Frustrations Out in the Open

Career and Education. There are still a fair number of women who are full-time, stay-at-home mothers and love every minute of it. However, that number is far smaller than it used to be a few generations ago. Many mothers in our generation went to college and began a career, and then left it all to stay at home with the children. While this decision is often in response to a clear call from God and best for the family, it can still be frustrating to think of the time and money lost on pursuing a career. And frankly, some of us really miss the workplace and the friends we had there.

Even for those of us who do work full- or part-time, the career path is never the same as our colleagues who are childless. Working mothers cannot make their jobs their first priority, and that can cause a lot of stress at home and at work. You can sit in the same work environment with the same educations and the same expectations, but no one is going to say that the job is the same for you as it is for non-parents.

Even the mothers who planned lifelong careers of full-time homemaking will probably confess that real life is different than they had anticipated. Some of us feel guilty when we realize that the job isn't nearly as enjoyable as it should be. We know other mothers would trade anything to be home with their children, and here we are, ungrateful. Being a mother is difficult work, no matter what your employment situation may be.

Marriage. I vaguely remember the years before our first child was born. Our days consisted mostly of working for eight hours, coming home, and then deciding what restaurant we wanted to bless with our presence. Now my husband works ten-hour days so I can work three-hour days. Except my three-hour days are more like twelve-hour days because clean laundry does not fall out of the sky.

Our time together as a married couple has changed, our money has disappeared, and our expectations of one another have skyrocketed. He's no longer that wonderful man who keeps me warm at night and made me the beneficiary of his life insurance. He's that wonderful man who keeps a roof over our heads and food on the table. He's the mechanic who can fix the car we need to drive to school tomorrow. He's the only other adult in the house when I run out of patience and have to turn the parenting over to someone else for a while. (For the record, he still keeps me warm at night, and I'm still the beneficiary of his life insurance.)

In his eyes, I'm the only person in the house who can create an actual meal out of food found in a grocery store. Without me, he and the children would starve or live on macaroni and cheese. He can't tell if a child is too sick to go to church, and there's no way he could plan a birthday party for six little girls.

We desperately need one another, in ways that neither of us could have ever fathomed. We have some friends who are going through a divorce, and we're watching their family melt into a puddle of legal details. In our distress at our friends' loss, Eric and I have formed a pact: if either of us should ever leave, the remaining partner has full rights to pack up the children, track down the offending spouse, and move right back in with them. There is no leaving this marriage now! The children have made us reaffirm the need for commitment, and as a result we are growing into better and more thoughtful spouses.

Travel (and Other Life-Long Dreams). I'm not going to lie; I want to see the world: Rome, Slovenia, London, Mexico, San Francisco. You name it; I have it on my list. So does my husband. We love to travel together but have somehow spawned two children who cannot ride in a car for more than five minutes without thinking that they are being cruelly mistreated. They love to visit new places, they adore hotels with elevators, and they are crazy to go to Disney. As long as these places are not outside a forty-mile drive from Kalamazoo, that is. You have to understand—this isn't an issue of vacation. This is a deep-seated desire that Eric and I share, and it's not working out like we had hoped. The Clemence personal dream might not be your personal dream, but I don't doubt that you've given up something special too.

Time. Oh, free time! Sweet, elusive, free time. Do you remember it? I remember having pots of it. I did crafts; I made money; I had a clean house. Of course I wouldn't trade my kids for an entire year of free time, and I realize that the time I have with them is precious and brief. I will have time in the future for hobbies and volunteering, but now I have to focus on the jobs God has given me for the present: teaching, loving, and caring for two fabulous little people. But there are still times when I walk slowly through the craft store and remember when an entire portion of my life was dedicated to my hobbies.

Finances. I know I've touched on this a few times already, but it's such a big topic that we need to discuss it thoroughly. Kids cost money. Lots and lots of money. From the moment you buy the pregnancy test until the moment your lawyer reads your will and testament, your money belongs to your children in some way or another. I keep thinking that each new age will bring a better financial situation, but so far I've been wrong. We grew out of formula and diapers and into field trips, camp, and ballet lessons. In the distance I can see braces, car insurance, and college looming with very large price tags. The expenses are endless!

Accepting the Reality and Making the Best of It

Okay, now that we've thoroughly discussed all of these concerns, limitations, and surprises, let's move on. We accept that this life is different than we had planned. This does not mean that we can sit around and let it overwhelm us. We have to take this challenge, make the best of it, and be the best parents we can be. We have to dig into God's Word to find the best possible way to honor God in this life He has given to us!

Galatians 2:20 says, "I have been crucified with Christ and I no longer live, but Christ lives in me. The life I live in the body, I live by faith in the Son of God, who loved me and gave himself for me." That is *such* a powerful reminder of our motivation. Christ set the ultimate example when He died for us. During His ministry He spent His time healing the sick and teaching the lost. He loved the unlovable, and He died for us while we were still sinners. He did not build a cozy house and make life comfortable for himself. If He could live and then die for us, we can certainly make the necessary sacrifices for the good of our children.

I have to remind myself continually that my life is not about *me*. It's not about *my* comfort or pleasure. It's about taking the gifts I have been given and spreading God's love to the best of my ability. I am a servant of God, my husband, my children, my church, and my community. Parenting has been God's most effective way to drill that lesson into my head. I'm thankful that parenting helps me mature and grow into the person God wants me to be.

It Comes Back Around

Sacrificing ourselves for the good of our children over decades is a unique experience in God's creation. Most of us understand the basics of animal parenting—we get the mating, the birthing, and the feeding. But then most animals just kick the kids out into the world after a relatively short time. The baby birds get tossed out of nests; the mama cat runs away to the farm next door. You never see all the mama cows helping at a birthday party or slaving away over forty cupcakes for soccer practice.

This emotional connection we have is unreasonable; it goes beyond physical needs or logic. Have you ever stopped to think about it? Why do we love our children? Why would a woman run into a burning building to get her baby, or put her career on hold to become a stay-at-home mother? Why would we give our kids anything they need at our own detriment?

I think God designed parenting this way to teach us about His unreasonable love for us. He goes beyond providing food

21

and a planet that will sustain our lives. He loves us so much that He wants a real relationship with us. He even gave us the free will to choose to disobey and ignore Him! And yet He loves us even in our disobedience.

I believe we have a greater understanding of that love when we look at our children. Parenting teaches us about unreasonable love and compassion, kindness and gentleness. This kind of love makes no sense, but it's within us anyway. You talk to any woman who has a three-week-old baby. She is covered in spit-up. She has averaged three hours of sleep for twenty-one days. She can't remember her own phone number or what panty hose are for. She wouldn't take this abuse (for lack of a better word) for anything else. If her husband kept her up all night and spit up on her five times a day she'd ask him to move to the garage. If her job demanded that she swell up to three times her regular size and endure intense physical pain for twenty-one hours, she'd never sign the contract. Motherhood isn't a reasonable experience.

But it gives us some perspective when God tells us He loves us. He sent His own Son to die for us because He loves us so much, and now we have a better understanding of how much He sacrificed and the depth of His love for us. Some of us are tempted to think, "Oh, no, Lord. I'm not that lovable. Look somewhere else." And our heavenly Father gently points to our dining room and says, "Well, you look at that four-year-old you have at the table. He's covered in ketchup and smashed peas, and he smells like Play-Doh and dirt. You love him like nuts. And I feel the same way about you." God wants us to understand His unreasonable love for us, His tenderness, His kindness and gentleness. As we feel this toward our own children, He teaches our hearts the same lessons.

A Lesson about Sheep

God's love for us prompts Him to protect us and provide for us when we are at our most vulnerable. In the Bible, Jesus used the examples of sheep to teach His followers about God's love and protection. Now, I'm no farmer or expert on animals. I've been around a few sheep, but that's because I live in a rural community and we've all been around a few sheep. I do know that sheep are sweet and kind of dumb. They provide wool for nice sweaters and eat a lot of grass. They need a lot of protection because they don't have any defenses like claws or stingers or even sharp teeth. They can't climb trees, and fluffy wool is a horrible camouflage. They need a shepherd to take care of them.

In Bible times, it was a manly career to watch the sheep. Because they were valued as part of a family's wealth, it was important to keep them safe. A shepherd couldn't fall asleep and let animals kill the flock, nor tend to his own priorities and forget they were there. It was a job that required care and dedication. Jesus said in John 10:11–15:

> "I am the good shepherd. The good shepherd lays down his life for the sheep. The hired hand is not the shepherd who owns the sheep. So when he sees the wolf coming, he abandons the sheep and runs away. Then the wolf attacks the flock and scatters it. The man runs away because he is a hired hand and cares nothing for the sheep. I am the good shepherd; I know my sheep and my sheep know me—just as the Father knows me and I know the Father—and I lay down my life for the sheep."

If Jesus taught about this idea today, He might have said: "I am the good parent. A good parent lays down his life for his kids. A babysitter doesn't have a real connection, so when hard times come the sitter runs out. I am the good parent, I know my kids and my kids know me, just like I know the heavenly Father and He knows me. I would die for my children."

I know we all pick our babysitters with care, but a hired attendant will take only so much before she calls the emergency numbers to order us home. And if our children are sick (or some other catastrophe develops), we wouldn't expect her to want to stay! Not only do we understand why she wants to leave, we are already looking for our coats and purses to get home as fast as possible. At the moment when she is running out, we are running in. It doesn't matter how much we were enjoying that dinner or movie or day at work, we give it up because our kids need us.

Very few of us will be called to die for our children's sakes, but I don't doubt we'd do it in an instant if the situation required. But Jesus did die for us, even when we were at our most unlovable. When common sense would say to rush out, Jesus rushed in. The Good Shepherd laid down His life for the sheep.

Let's look at Romans 8:14–17, which says,

> Those who are led by the Spirit of God are sons of God. For you did not receive a spirit that makes you a slave again to fear, but you received the Spirit of sonship. And by him we cry, "Abba, Father." The Spirit himself testifies with our spirit that we are God's children. Now if we are children, then we are heirs—heirs of God and co-heirs with Christ, if indeed we share in his sufferings in order that we may also share in his glory.

It takes a special relationship to become an heir. For example, the older neighbors across the street have become our friends.

We occasionally enjoy their company over a meal and use their hill for sledding. They bring our kids Christmas gifts and Easter baskets and invite us to enjoy the hobby train track in their basement. But we don't expect to inherit anything when they eventually pass away. We care for one another, but our relationship isn't so deep that we would share in their inheritance.

As Christians, we do share in God's inheritance because He has made us His children! While we were strangers to Him, He offered us a chance to become a permanent part of His family by giving us His Spirit and adopting us. We have a few friends who have adopted children, and I marvel at what God does for their families. Parents look out at a sea of faces and say, "You. Right there. I want you to be part of my family." The legal formalities bring them into the same relationship as children who are naturally born into the family.

We can call God "Abba, Father" because He offers us the Spirit of sonship. Through Christ's death on the cross, we can be part of God's family. Because God is a loving and good parent, He made the sacrifice that was needed to include us and give us rights of inheritance.

The Ultimate Example of Selflessness

Because of God's example, we can learn to make the sacrifices necessary to be good moms. No one warned me about the volume of sacrifices ahead of time. I distinctly remember a few smiles on faces when I was pregnant, and now I realize those people were thinking, "This poor fool has no idea of what she's about to experience." And they were right. I had no idea. I did not know I could cling to my husband with such fierce panic at the thought of parenting alone. I had no idea that I wouldn't complete a craft project for eight years. I did not realize that a week at camp costs more than a monthly car payment.

But I also didn't realize the love I could feel for my children. I didn't realize I could hold a sick, feverish little person and worry more for his health than my own. No one could have made me understand that I would be glad to plan a trip to Disney for their sakes, rather than a trip to Rome. There's no way to explain the connection between a parent and child. It's a miraculous gift, just like the connection between God and His children.

Because we are God's children, He died to protect us, and shares His inheritance with us. He feels that strongly about our worth. He values us! And if ever you doubt it, go take a look at that four-year-old in the dining room. He's pretending to eat his peas and he really needs a bath. But you would die for him on the spot.

God loves you like that.

Study Questions

1. What sacrifice stings the most? Is this something you can reclaim in the years to come, or is there a way you can still make it work after you tweak your dream a bit? If there is no way to make it work, have you made your peace with it? How have you changed since letting this go?

2. Did anyone teach you how to be selfless, or are you learning this for the first time? What do you still need to learn in this area?

3. Do you truly believe that God loves and values you? How does your life reflect that belief or disbelief?
4. For further study, read Matthew 7:9–11; Colossians 3:12–14; Titus 2:3–5.

WHAT IS THE KINDEST THING YOUR MOTHER EVER DID FOR YOU?

- My mother was a seamstress in the 70s, and when I was fifteen she sewed about twenty polyester leisure suits to sell so I could buy an AKC registered cocker spaniel to show at dog shows! —Barb

- One word . . . adoption! I can't imagine the person I may have been if I had not been adopted into such a loving, Christian home. —Sandy

- She came alongside me and affirmed me as I mothered my own children. —Sara

- After I had been dating for a short while, my mother came to me and told me that if I ever got pregnant I was always welcome at home. This was in the 60s, when teenage pregnancy still carried quite a stigma. —Karen

- My mother prayed with us, kept a clean house, and taught us the Bible. She was always home for us. —Grandma Freda

- During my husband's last surgery she dropped everything and flew down to be with us. I needed my mom and she was there! —Melody

- She loved me unconditionally and introduced me to Jesus. —Melissa

- My mom worked a non-glamorous, physically strenuous job to help provide for our family. She did it for over thirty years without much complaining at all. —Jenny

- When I was nineteen I hit a garbage truck and totaled my mother's new car. She picked me up from the emergency room, took me home, and kissed my forehead right above where I had smashed my face into the steering wheel. And then she patiently started calling the insurance companies while I slept off the pain killers. —Jessie

CHAPTER 2

I Want to Be a Patient Mother

Wednesday, 6:53 a.m.: My son and I were standing in the kitchen, discussing the snack he wanted to take to kindergarten for his Leader Day. The conversation went in circles as we struggled to reach a decision that made us both happy. I closed my eyes, willing myself to not start shouting. My seven-year-old daughter, eating her breakfast at the table, saw me gathering my patience and yelled, "Be strong, Mother. Be strong!" Her accurate assessment of the situation made me laugh out loud. I *did* need to be strong, because Caleb wasn't trying to confuse or irritate me; he just can't make a decision quickly or easily. I needed all the patience I had in my body just to get through one conversation.

Did any of us truly realize how impatient we were before we had children? I can deal with almost any kind of person. Truly, I can. I used to think this qualified me as patient. The problem is that I can deal with the difficult ones for only about five minutes. I'll never forget the day when I was a young social worker, working in the foster care system in southwest Michigan. I was responsible for driving a biological father home from his weekly visit with his children, who had been placed in foster care. I had met him briefly; he was a pretty nice guy. I didn't think that driving him the thirty minutes from the agency to his house would be a big deal.

I am not kidding when I say that halfway through the drive I almost pulled over to the side of the road and handed him the keys to my personal car. I would rather have walked ten miles back to Hartford on a lonely country road than spend fifteen more minutes in a car with that man. He rambled, and whined, and blamed everyone else for every mess he was in. I had no more patience for him.

If I could barely survive a half hour in a car with an emotionally fragile man, how do you think I have fared the 87,600 hours I've been a mother? I assure you that my lack of patience came as quite a shock. I had assumed that this man was an aberrant example; surely I was still a patient woman. It turns out that I'm not at all a patient woman, and motherhood has taught me this. Parents experience a wide range of situations that require us to control our emotions and choose our words well. Whether these situations are caused by our children's natural immaturity or their poor choices, we must respond to them patiently.

A Sapling in a Hurricane of Five-Year-Olds

Proving God's everlasting sense of humor, I finished writing the preceding paragraph *yesterday*. I was alone in my room typing away about patience. This morning God had me actually experience the need for it firsthand. I work part-time at my kids' elementary school, where I'm a teacher's aide in a large first grade classroom. The kids were wound up because it was Friday, and their teacher (the adult in the class with actual child-management skills *and* patience) was in the hallway giving progress testing. This left me, alone, in a room with the remaining twenty-seven children.

Three of these children were working quietly and steadily. Five of them needed help understanding their assignment, all at the same time. The rest of them simultaneously came up with ingenious ways to drive me mad. These attempts ranged from wandering around the room to patting my bottom while saying, "Mrs.Clemence-Mrs.Clemence-Mrs. Clemence-Mrs.Clemence." I contemplated hiding in a closet, but the room didn't have one big enough to fit me.

Finally the teacher sensed my distress (she could hear me yelling from the hall) and came in to rescue me. I spent an hour doing paperwork to regain my wits before heading to my son's kindergarten class, which had a substitute teacher. Now, my son's class is a bit wild on a good day, when the teacher is there to enforce the rules the kids have been practicing for six months. You can imagine what ensues when a well-meaning but woefully unprepared sub walks through the door. The poor woman was a sapling in a hurricane of five-year-olds. She didn't have a chance. I spent an hour serving as crowd control before the twenty-two of them were herded to lunch. By the time I left for home I was an emotional puddle. Whatever patience I had when I woke up had been worn to a nub. I was a nub.

Did the children do this on purpose? No, they did not. They were just being children. They don't have fully developed social skills, so they don't realize how impolite it is to pat an adult's bottom and say her name five times. They don't have fully developed brains, so they need help understanding how to divide compound words. They don't yet have complete control over their little bodies, so they may have to dash to the bathroom at the last second. Their egos still demand that the world revolves around them, so fairness, sharing, and consideration for others are iffy subjects. It's up to us adults to teach them and to make sure they can grow into mature adults. This takes patience on our part.

One small, simple verse puts this into correct perspective for me: "Nobody should seek his own good, but the good of others" (1 Corinthians 10:24). When a child frustrates me, I need to step back and think, "What will be best for this child right now? What does he need?" Obviously a kid who has just wet his pants for the third time does not need me shouting over him in a rage. My shouting is not going to fix anything. The fix is getting a grip on myself and finding a fourth pair of pants. And of course I need to talk with him about how important it is to stop playing to get to the potty in time, and we need to set up regular potty breaks throughout the day. All of this can be done firmly and calmly. Eventually the lesson will be learned and we'll move on to our next challenge of maturity.

Catching Flies with Honey

A few days ago my son ran into the kitchen and looked at my dinner preparations. He announced, "Mom, this is such a good dinner! I don't hate it!" I sighed and said, "Yes, Cabo, I know. Usually I try to make dinners you hate, but this is what we're having tonight." The monkey looked at me with a little grin and said, "I know what's wrong wif you, Mom. You're always trying to make my food bad." This is the boy's backward way of complimenting dinner and making a little joke. We're working on learning better compliments and funnier jokes.

We connect with people through our words. But what we say rarely matters as much as how we say it. Proverbs 15:1 says, "A gentle answer turns away wrath, but a harsh word stirs up anger." Proverbs 25:15 says, "Through patience a ruler can be persuaded, and a gentle tongue can break a bone." If I truly care about a person, I need to respond to him or her with gentleness and patience. And that patience will make a profound difference. It can bring grace and joy to even the most difficult place.

It's no secret that a kind word can pivot circumstances as if by magic. Most of us are familiar with the scenario of being lost in a different city with an irritated spouse. Tensions run high. The driver is operating a huge hunk of steel at high speeds in unfamiliar territory. Exits are whizzing by, locals are honking and gesturing wildly, and the kids are asking inane questions from the backseat. If the navigator says even one word about this being the driver's fault, all is lost right then. It's Giant Fight time. You might as well stop the car and ask to move into a stranger's house.

Last spring our family drove to New Jersey to visit some friends. This drive takes fifty-two hours and is twelve thousand miles long. (Okay, it's really only eleven hours and seven hundred miles. But you get my point.) On our way home, Eric had finally gotten tired enough to let me drive. We were so close to the end of the toll road that we could almost see the exit to I-69. But I didn't understand Eric's directions and

I missed our exit because I thought we still had another mile. Do you know how many miles it is between exits on the toll road? Many, many miles. My husband stared dumbfounded at the map, and then looked up at me. He opened his mouth and said, "Ah."

There you go, my friends. That was the pivot that redirected what could have been a horrible fight. He said, "Ah." And he looked back down at the map and calmly found a different way home, which involved twenty extra miles in Indiana and a winding, snaky trip through southern Michigan until we drove out of a cornfield and into our town. My husband is a patient man by nature, so I wasn't too surprised. But I was thankful for his kind word, which made me feel better when I'd made a dumb mistake.

I know it wasn't just his patience that controlled his tongue. It's because he loves me. When we love a person, we see his or her worth and act accordingly. Eric would have been justified to snap at me; he was tired and had driven through most of Ohio and some of Pennsylvania. What would have been a thirty-minute end to our trip took an hour and a half. But because he loves me, he controlled his tongue. When we love someone, we choose to be patient even when our frustration is valid.

If we choose to be unkind, our words can wound deeply. Even when we speak the truth, if we do not speak it in a way that shows that we see the person as valuable, we wound them. When our child asks about dinner, we may say, "I don't know what we're eating yet." A gentle tone implies that we just don't know what's for dinner. But a harsh tone says, "If you weren't so annoying, you wouldn't have bothered me with that stupid question." We don't try to hurt what is valuable to us.

My kids remind me of this all the time with their own tones of voice and attitudes. If my daughter comes to me at 6:00 a.m. and asks for socks, how she asks is going to make all the difference. "Mom, you didn't wash my socks again," is not going to go well for her. But, "Mom, do I have any clean socks in the dryer?" has the same meaning without the implication that I am a lazy and negligent sock manager. The truth is that I am often a terrible laundress. But nobody needs to point that out to me; I know it.

When we choose to be calm and gentle with our children's mistakes and immaturity, we show them we love and value them. So I will calmly discipline my children as needed, without reminding them that they made this mistake four hundred times this year. I will not heave a huge sigh when my son asks me to tie his shoe, again. I will slowly kill off my selfish nature one situation at a time, by reminding myself that God loves these precious small people. It's not their fault that they are still developing and need help. It's not his fault that he has bad dreams and wakes me up five times a night. It's not her fault that she can't fold shirts neatly and her dresser looks like a bomb site. They are doing the best they can. And when they *aren't* doing the best they can, I will deal with it gently, without spreading verbal poison through our family.

Stop Poking Your Sister!

A kid can't help the fact that she's young or little or un-taught. But a child has total control over provoking the people around her. This is what happens when you've patiently explained something once or twice—enough to convey your expectations—and then, just to goad, annoy, or defy everyone, the little one does it anyway. We see this in little behaviors like kicking the back of the driver's seat or poking his sister, and in bigger things like "forgetting" to take out the trash again or asking twelve times for a candy bar at the checkout.

When a child provokes us, we need to have the patience to keep our emotions in check. No screaming, smacking, degrading, or insulting the child. Ephesians 4:26 teaches that in our anger we cannot sin. If our words are full of bitterness, rage, or malice, we're sinning. We have to choose different words.

Does this mean that a good mother never yells at her kids? I don't think it does. In our previous example of a boy wetting his pants repeatedly, a mother needs to get a grip on herself. Shouting over an innocent mistake (no matter how annoying it may be) is not helpful. But in my personal opinion, when a child behaves badly on purpose, a raised voice might be appropriate. A raised voice isn't going to hurt anyone, but as we discussed, words hurled in anger with a desire to destroy will kill a small soul. So, are we communicating our deep displeasure at a loud volume, or are we losing our frustrations in an angry, ugly tirade? There's a big difference.

My friend Jenny, a ridiculously patient woman, gave me this example about losing it:

> The thing that pushes my buttons most is when the kids completely ignore me when I am talking to them. I mean complete, total, outright, blatant disobedience. I feel the anger and frustration building up inside of me. I remain patient and think I'm doing okay, and then all of a sudden I start yelling. It's like it comes from my toes, runs up through my body, and spits out of my mouth. Then as soon

as I say it I want to take it back. Not because I feel bad that they got into trouble or are being punished, but because of my reaction to the situation. I generally save my "snapping" for home. I can think of one time I lost it in the store and remember thinking, "Oh my, I've become one of *those* mothers!" It was an eye-opener for me. I could hear myself and I didn't like it at all. There have been a few times when I could see the hurt in my girls' eyes. They quietly did what I wanted but I felt badly at how I motivated them to do it.

I know without a doubt that Jenny isn't alone in her experience. It isn't that the kids don't need correction, because they do. But how we do it makes a big difference. When we feel the emotions of anger or irritation at being provoked, we must not retaliate by tearing down the other person.

Let Us Not Spew

Now that we've discussed the need, we need specific directions on what to say and how to say it. Paul writes in his letter to the Ephesians:

> Do not let any unwholesome talk come out of your mouths, but only what is helpful for building others up according to their needs, that it may benefit those who listen . . . Get rid of all bitterness, rage, and anger, brawling and slander, along with every form of malice. Be kind and compassionate to one another, forgiving each other, just as in Christ God forgave you. (4:29, 31–32)

Do our words build up our children? Are they encouraging and beneficial? Does our child know she is loved after we've said our part? I know at times we must have difficult conversations with our kids, and they will be angry or upset with us. But we can still season those hard moments with kindness and forgiveness. Healthy discipline addresses the behavior and situation while allowing our kids to know that we still love them.

Beneficial communication will not contain bitterness, anger, slander, or malice. I know that sometimes we feel all of those things, and often the source of our problem isn't even our children. We may be angry at our finances, or the school system, or our neighbors. And then one of the kids comes in the kitchen and asks for fruit snacks and we yell at them about tooth decay and childhood obesity. Not only does our child feel bad for the world's problems, but she also is mad because she still doesn't have any fruit snacks. We've solved nothing and made our kid feel bad.

I'd like to identify one small phrase in these verses that makes a huge difference. It says to build others up "according to *their needs*." How do we know what a person needs? We can't know unless we are paying close attention to him or her. It takes long-term study to really know a person, and then to match our words to our child's heart. Once we know what our child needs, then we can do our best to meet those needs.

So let's study our children! Let's know their personalities, strengths, and weaknesses. Let's find out who they are and use our words to teach them, encourage them, discipline them, and love them as we bring out the best in them.

This Has Been Painful; Can We Talk About Something Else Now?

Okay, my friends. How patient are you feeling right now? I am currently feeling like a heel. Do you remember the example about how we shouldn't yell at the child who has wet his pants for the third time? I need to be honest. That happened in my house, and I failed big time. I yelled. I hollered. I whacked my head on the wall. I tell you this story in hopes that you are doing better than I did.

However, I am happy to report that I haven't made this mistake in nearly three years. Yes, that particular child has matured out of the behavior, but so have I. Thanks to God's grace, I have far more patience than I ever knew existed. And you, too, can have this blessing. May God teach you about His patience as He continues to teach me.

Study Questions

1. Are you a patient person? Do your kids agree with this assessment?
2. What makes you lose your patience the fastest?
3. Do you secretly feel like your own mother leaves your house, goes home, and laughs for hours? Do you suspect she thinks you deserve the children you have because of your own behavior as a child? How often did you test your mother's patience when you were young?
4. For further study, read Proverbs 19:11; Romans 5:3–5; 1 Timothy 1:15–17.

WHAT DO YOU DO WHEN YOU NEED TIME TO YOURSELF?

- I love walking outdoors. —Sara

- I lock myself in the bathroom. I take my book and just sit and read. —Jenny

- I get up earlier or stay up later than everyone else. —Sara (a different Sara—I know a lot of Saras)

- When the girls were small, I took a warm bath with a good book. —Melissa

- I like to scrapbook, read, and sew. —Melody

- It was years before I ever had time for myself. Now I have lots of time for myself. —Grandma Freda

- Go for a walk. I used to go to the supermarket, but now the people there wear me out faster than my children. —Shana

- When I had younger kids at home, every Friday night their dad would take them to the university gym or pool and give me a chance to be alone. —Barb

- It depends on whether or not I need to also hide or escape! Sometimes I shop, walk, visit with friends, or e-mail. I also have hobbies: sewing, crocheting, making Christmas presents, reading. —Deb

CHAPTER 3

I Want to Be a Peaceful and Well-Balanced Mother

Have you spent time with another mother who has a wonderful, confident groove to her life? She isn't prideful, but neither does she wallow in insecurity or fear that she is a bad mother. She is comfortable with the choices she has made for her family, but she doesn't look down on those who have chosen differently. Her kids are happy and well-behaved, but not so well-behaved that you feel weird around them. She is happy to help others when they need her, but she doesn't feel like she has to be everyone's doormat. She has hobbies and interests that make her fun to be around, and she has enough energy to contribute to the community.

In contrast, have you ever been around a mother who has no peace in her soul? She may be overly fearful, aggressive, protective, or irritable. Perhaps she has unattainably high standards, or she is so overwhelmed that she has withdrawn socially. These women are out of balance in many aspects of their life, both as individuals and as mothers. While their actions seem reasonable to themselves, others sense that lack of peace and shy away from them.

Obviously, we want to be at peace with ourselves, others, and God. But how does a woman find that peace? Balance occurs when we have an understanding of our gifts, healthy boundaries with other people, and a deep relationship with God. When we take the time to develop these areas, our lives and families will be blessed by the calm that defines our lives.

I Think I'd Be Better at This If I Were Someone Else

When a woman doesn't understand her unique gifts and talents, she is without an anchor in her mothering soul. Think about it—how many times have you come home feeling completely undone after an outing with other mothers? You sit and compare and drive yourself crazy. "Jenny is so patient with her girls; maybe I should not be so hasty with my kids." "Deb homeschools five children; maybe I should have more kids and homeschool, too." "Kris adopted two children from Ethiopia; maybe I'm being selfish by raising only two biological kids." "Kara works full-time and has two boys; maybe I should get a job with a bigger paycheck." Or, "Shana hasn't worked outside the house in seven years; maybe I'm being selfish by needing time away from the kids each week."

These are actual thoughts I've had about my friends. These women are amazing people! I love them to bits, but I often feel insecure when I compare myself to them and come out lacking. I've had to work to come to peace with the fact that I am not any of them. I don't have their strengths, I don't share their every goal, and God has a different plan for each of our lives. I could not homeschool my children for more than three days before all of us would be in tears. Audrey would be begging for friends, Caleb would be systematically tearing the house into pieces in the name of "science," and I would be hiding in the closet, rocking myself quietly. An epic disaster, if ever there was one. Instead, I have learned to be thankful for the things I do well as a mother, like being involved in their schooling and teaching them to have a sense of humor.

Do you know your talents as a mother, and are you confident enough to use them? Maybe you're a great teacher, or incredibly organized. Maybe you can spend hours on the floor playing games with the kids or have amazing craft ideas. Maybe you're so laid back that it doesn't bother you when ten little boys upend your home for the afternoon. Use your gifts with confidence! Be thankful you're unique and that your kids are unique, too. It will help cover the multitudes of areas where you might fall short.

I'm going to state the obvious—you will have friends with skills superior to yours in some areas. Someone's going to have a cleaner house. Someone's going to be more patient. Someone is going to inspire her children to academic excellence. Don't let this keep you up at night. If you struggle in a friend's area of expertise, learn what you can from her. In this way, you can continually become a better mother. However, don't beat yourself up over what you will never be able to do well. Let it go and focus on being good at who you are, which will make you the best mom you can be. Peaceful, well-balanced mothers know how to use their strengths to their full potential and allow grace to cover their weaknesses.

This Kid Needs a Book; That Kid Needs an Apron

While it's important to know yourself to stay balanced and find peace, it's also important to pay close attention to your children's personalities and individual needs. Actions or activities important to one child may not communicate love at all to another child. My daughter and I love to read together. We snuggle up and read chapter books. Caleb loves to read, too, but he's happiest when we're engaged in some kind of chore together. He gets out the brooms and mops when I'm cooking so he can "clean" while I'm working. Then he demands to deliver food to the table so he can be the waiter. Audrey loves to snuggle; Caleb loves to work. I've learned to focus my time with each kid based on his or her preferences.

Knowing our talents and our children's personalities and interests helps us find meaningful ways to connect with our kids. As an added benefit, you'll feel more confident as a mother because your efforts at connecting with each child, one-on-one, are likely to be well received.

We don't have to be all-around perfect mothers. No mother can do it all just right, all the time. We're not perfect, our mothers weren't perfect, and even that woman behind you in the carpool lane—she's not perfect either. And you know what? That's okay, because none of us are raising perfect kids. Let's find peace with our imperfections and simply do the best we can.

You're Not Okay, but I'm Not Okay Either

If we must learn to be gracious with our own shortcomings, we must also learn to be gracious with the shortcomings of our friends. Since none of us are perfect mothers, I beg that we cut one another some slack. This is an area where I fall painfully short. Occasionally it frustrates me when I see mothers do things differently than I would do them. Sometimes this bothers me because I have to deal with their resulting badly behaved children. Sometimes this bothers me because of my own insecurities. And other times it bothers me because I can really be a self-righteous moron. It's not pretty, but it's the truth.

The Holy Spirit continually convicts me when I start to criticize my friends and their parenting styles. Criticizing is not helpful or edifying to anyone. I clearly remember a group road trip with a person who spent the time finding fault with any decision she didn't get to make. She hated the restaurant. The schedule did not please her. She did not like our route. At one point she (mercifully) fell asleep for several hours. When she awoke the first words out of her mouth were, "We're lost, aren't we?" The rest of us wanted to leave her at a truck stop. When we allow our minds to dwell on the negative, we agitate ourselves and those around us.

We're put here to encourage and help one another, not criticize or grade each other on a subjective scale. Romans 14:4 says, "Who are you to judge someone else's servant? To his own master he stands or falls. And he will stand, for the Lord is able to make him stand." We need to be available to our friends when they need us, whether that is with advice, fellowship, or service. But we must realize that God alone will judge; we are not in charge of our friends and their parenting responsibilities. And while mothers can help one another in a multitude of ways, it is God who teaches us each the way to go when we don't know what to do for our children. It is God who gives us strength to continue when we're out of energy. And it will be God who directs our children one day on their own journeys through life. Humility demands that we do not elevate ourselves to a position that only God is qualified to have.

Peace comes with encouragement, not criticism. Have you ever noticed a friend's gift or talent and then commented on it? Next time you notice, speak up and say, "Hey, you have the greatest craft projects for your kids!" Then watch a little stress ease out of your friend's shoulders. God calls us to share His peace by encouraging one another.

I Refuse to Answer You While I Am Engaged in Bathroom Activities

As a human being, I really enjoy having certain times all to myself—like when I have to use the bathroom. Therefore, when I am sitting quietly in the bathroom and I hear little footsteps come up to the door, I hold my breath, hoping the short person will go away and leave me in peace. I hear the little person breathing on the other side of the door, straining to hear any noise that would indicate that I am in residence. It's a silent, drawn out game of waiting. Finally the child will yell, "Um, Mom?" And I'll sigh and mutter, "What?!" Then there will be a long pause while the kid realizes that whatever he or she asks for will be denied. "Never mind!" the child says, and eases away from the door. This is repeated many times each week in our house and in millions of houses around the world.

Some of us would really enjoy some quiet time to think, pray, and be responsible for only ourselves. I'll never forget the year my son was born. Eric and I had decided that with two kids I would be a full-time stay-at-home mother, so I quit my job as the church secretary four months before Caleb was born. Audrey and I stayed home and entertained each other. She would climb into bed with me at 5:30 each morning and say, "Mamma, do now? Do now, Mamma?" She wanted my company from 5:30 a.m. to 8:00 p.m. I found that I wasn't that great of a companion for her.

Eight months after I had given up my job at church, my replacement quit with no notice. Our minister called and asked me to come back to work just a few hours each week until they could find another replacement. I remember that first day back at work as clearly as it was yesterday. I sat in my quiet office, gripping a mug of hot coffee. I said to myself and God, *"I will never leave again."* Although eventually I did change jobs, it was years later. This simple decision by my husband and me made a huge impact on my mental health and turned out to be a big blessing to our family.

So, how do *you* get time to yourself? Maybe you're the kind of mom who doesn't need all that much personal space. My dear step-grandmother, Freda, grew up in a house with many children, and when she got married she found herself terribly lonely. So she had a baby ten months after her wedding, and then eight more kids followed. She said the biggest shock of motherhood was when all the kids left home and her house was empty again. Even to this day she's happiest with lots of people and children around.

Some mothers thrive in this kind of close environment, and good for you all. (See, I've been practicing what I've learned in the last section!) The rest of us need to establish boundaries to have time to ourselves on a regular basis. Does wanting time to ourselves make us selfish? No, not if we do it in the right way for the right reasons. For example, backpacking around Europe alone this summer is probably a bad idea. Your kids need you, and you know your husband won't have any clean socks if you leave for three months. We have to establish boundaries in ways that make sense for our families. They should also fulfill a purpose, such as allowing us to recharge to continue to meet our family's needs.

Even Jesus needed a break from the crowds. Matthew chapter 14 relates one such incident. In the beginning of the chapter Jesus' beloved cousin was killed by King Herod. After John's death, Matthew relates that "when Jesus heard what had happened, he withdrew by boat privately to a solitary place" (v. 13). As a human, Jesus needed some time alone. He needed a break from the crowds to grieve. He needed some space to prepare himself to handle the next onslaught of needs.

When the crowd found out where He was, they followed Him on foot. (Is this sounding familiar to anyone?) Jesus had compassion on them, so He healed their sick. The disciples pointed out that the huge crowd was hungry, so Jesus fed them all. (Still sounding like your life? It sounds like mine, except for the miracle dinner for five thousand.) Then Jesus sent the disciples in a boat to the other side of the lake, and He went up a mountain for some private time to pray (finally!).

When He was refreshed and ready to join His friends, He walked out on the water to meet them where they waited in the boat. Later, when Jesus's boat reached Gennesaret, the people thronged around Him, begging for healing and grabbing at His clothes. The chaos and endless needs drove Jesus to spend time alone. I think all mothers know to a lesser degree how Jesus felt, and I think we are wise to provide ourselves the same respite.

Good Fences Make Good Neighbors

I don't have the greatest fence around my property. There is a fence, of sorts. It's an ancient wire thing that has rusted and runs through the middle of many trees. To replace it we'd have to hire a tree cutter and an excavator. Because we do not have several thousand dollars lying around for fence replacement, we put up with what we have. While the fence keeps out most animals and gives our kids safe limits, it does nothing to give us privacy. Our neighbors can stare out their back windows right into our kitchen. Luckily the neighborhood has been respectful of this open view, and most of us keep things relatively clean and tidy. I mean, I can't actually see anybody's Trans Am up on blocks behind their garage, if you consider that tidy.

The truth of the human condition is that we have to respect one another's boundaries. We have to respect time and schedules, personality differences, and different values. What is important to *me* might not be important to *you*. What drives me crazy might not even register on your radar. The trick is communicating peacefully to each other about what we need the most, while remaining flexible about the rest of it.

Before a person can communicate her boundaries, she has to know what she needs as an individual. She has to clarify: "What do I expect of myself and what do I expect of you?" If a mother has been feeling particularly short-tempered, frazzled, and unbalanced lately, what's making her feel that way? Is it the children's behavior, the in-laws attempting to run her life, or her job encroaching on her personal life? These are just examples of how different people or responsibilities can overstep a boundary and make life miserable. Almost anyone or anything can become a problem if personal space is not respected.

Once we know who or what is causing the problem, then we need to identify what a balanced resolution to the problem looks like. I emphasize the word *balanced*. I don't care how stressful your relationship with your mother is, she is not going to move to Portugal next month to simplify your life. You have to find a way to love her gracefully while setting some boundaries. If your job is a problem, you probably don't have the luxury of quitting tomorrow. You have to deal with the issues until you can afford to quit without bankrupting your family.

So picture a happy resolution to this conflict that works for all parties involved. Perhaps your mother would stop spoiling your children if you explained your family's new behavior policy to her and asked her to help make it work. Maybe your boss would stop calling you at home if you took time to clarify details before you left each night. No matter what it is, give yourself the luxury of imagining how the situation would look if everyone was happy and working well together. Then carefully plot out small steps that might bring about this balance.

Even your small improvements might make a big difference. Get creative about solutions. To have some time to yourself during the week, swap babysitting services with a trusted friend. You could have Tuesday morning off, and she could have Thursdays. Or if you need adult conversation, join a mothering group like MOPS, which gives you fellowship and babysitting rolled into one great morning a few times each month. Maybe all you want to do is read a whole book. I'm assuming the kids go to bed earlier than you do, so ignore the piles of dishes and dirty laundry and make "Book Night" a reality a once a week. When the going gets really rough, just tell everyone that you're reading or sewing or whatever, and unless someone is bleeding or on fire, you are not to be disturbed.

They're safe, they have something to do, and they know you'll be in a better mood after having some time to yourself.

However, sometimes all the thinking, planning, and hinting in the world does not help. This is when you'll need to have the big, long, awkward conversation with the person who oversteps your boundaries. Sometimes there is just no way around it. But do your best to be prepared for the conversation. Pray before you speak. If possible, pray for several days before you bring up your concerns. Ask God for a gentle and humble way to address the problem. When the conversation occurs, explain why you need what you need, and then try to work with the person to make the solution a reality.

In life, there is bound to be conflict. The book of Proverbs addresses these situations repeatedly. It's not easy to meet our needs and the needs of those around us, especially when the needs are wildly different. The wise Solomon taught us the following truths that will guide us as we attempt to set respectful boundaries:

- "Reckless words pierce like a sword, but the tongue of the wise brings healing" (12:18).
- "A gentle answer turns away wrath, but a harsh word stirs up anger" (15:1).
- "A hot-tempered man stirs up dissension, but a patient man calms a quarrel" (15:18).

These truths teach that when we speak patiently, humbly, and wisely, our difficult conversation will go better than if we speak out of frustration, anger, or pride. If we dedicate our plan (and our attitude) to God, He can bring peace to the situation. "Commit to the Lord whatever you do, and your plans will succeed," taught Solomon (16:3).

When you pray for this conversation, ask God to show you your own motivations before you address the situation. Remember, Scripture doesn't teach that we can do whatever we want and then expect God to bless us. We have to make sure that what we want is what God wants. If our ways are pleasing to Him, then He will give us the humility, patience, and wisdom to succeed—in His time. Even after a lot of prayer a conversation can still go horribly wrong. The other person may be offended or get defensive. We can't control his or her response, only our own behavior and attitudes. But I believe that God will honor our desire to honor Him by helping us with the situation.

The Source of True, Lasting Peace

Finally, we need to discuss the source of true peace—a deep relationship with God. Without God filling our lives, any attempt we make at peace will be futile. A personal relationship with God occurs when we pray, study the Bible, and act in obedience to what we learn. Jesus promises to give us peace and keep our approach to life balanced. He said, "Peace I leave with you; my peace I give you. I do not give to you as the world gives. Do not let your hearts be troubled and do not be afraid" (John 14:27).

"Great!" we shout. "I want to be filled with God's peace. Now tell me how to do that." It's one of those grand spiritual concepts that we talk about on Sunday morning but then on Monday have no idea how to make it work on a practical, daily basis. It's so hard to have God's peace when you're up at 3 a.m. with a vomiting child, or the car battery is dead again, or your boss needs the report that was due last week. Where's God's peace in *that*?

Cynthia Heald, in her book *Becoming a Woman of Simplicity*, gives a clear answer to this problem. She writes, "We are kept in perfect peace, not only when we trust, but also when our thoughts are fixed on God. One way to keep our minds fixed on the Lord is to separate ourselves from the world for the sole purpose of sitting silently in His presence. These moments of solitude can be added to your Bible reading and prayer time or they can be a separate time set aside in order to listen to the Lord. All that is necessary is to be still and pray, 'Speak, Lord.'"

Another term for this time with God is *abiding*. Abiding in God means staying connected to Him at all times. Turn with me to John 15:5–12 where Jesus said,

"I am the vine; you are the branches. If a man remains in me and I in him, he will bear much fruit; apart from me you can do nothing. If anyone does not remain in me, he is like a branch that is thrown away and withers; such branches are picked up, thrown into the fire and burned. If you remain in me and my words remain in you, ask whatever you wish, and it will be given you. This is to my Father's glory, that you bear much fruit, showing yourselves to be my disciples. As the Father has loved me, so have I loved you. Now remain in my love. If you obey my commands, you will remain in my love, just as I have obeyed my Father's commands and remain in his love. I have told you this so that my joy may be in you and that your joy may be complete. My command is this: Love each other as I have loved you."

There is a wealth of God's wisdom in this small passage, but I'm going to focus on a few observations. First, Jesus said that we will bear fruit (and having His peace is part of bearing fruit) only when we remain in Him. Second, when we remain in Him, we can ask for whatever we need and it will be given to us. Third, remaining in His love is simple—we accomplish it by obeying His commands. And the most important command is that we love one another as He has loved us.

We can't know how He has loved us or how He wants us to love others without reading His words to us and praying for His guidance, so we must set aside time to spend with Him. As I mentioned above, Cynthia Heald recommends taking time after reading and praying to listen, to say, "Speak, Lord." When we ask Him to speak to us, the Holy Spirit will indeed answer. It just takes time and the discipline to wait and listen.

Personally, this discipline of listening took me a long time to develop. I'm getting better, but I still have a long way to go. Each day I try to listen for God to speak. Sometimes He does so, quickly and clearly. Sometimes He is silent, but I know that He is near and we sit in companionable silence. Never mind whether or not He speaks—let me assure you that the peace is *profound* when I sit quietly with God. I challenge you to try this for yourself. The blessings you and your family will reap as you seek God's peace will amaze you.

A Moment to Reflect

My friend, take a moment to reflect on the peace, or lack thereof, in your own life. Are you comfortable with yourself? Are you struggling to accept your friends and their choices? Think about the boundaries you have with others and how you could make them healthier. And finally, consider the peace deep in your soul. Is the deepest part of you filled with a calm assurance that you are pleasing God? Do you regularly read His Word, pray, and listen?

I pray that as you consider these areas, God will speak to your heart. May He encourage you in the areas you are doing well and gently instruct you in the areas where you are falling short. Claim this promise for your own life: "Peace I leave with you; my peace I give you. I do not give to you as the world gives. Do not let your hearts be troubled and do not be afraid" (John 14:27).

Study Questions

1. What behaviors do you see in mothers who lack peace? Think of examples from your own life and other mothers you have known.

2. What are your strengths, and how do they help you be a great mom?

3. What are your weaknesses, and how do you compensate for them?

4. Do you have any regular time to yourself? If not, how can you make time in the schedule? What will you do with that time?

5. Is anyone causing you problems by not respecting your personal space or time? What small steps can you take to change the situation? Also, carefully consider whether your behavior oversteps the personal space of a friend or family member. What can you do to change your own behavior?

6. For further study, read Isaiah 26:3; Romans 12:3–8; 1 Corinthians 7:7.

WHAT DO YOU DO WELL AS A MOTHER?

- I always carried through with my directions, even when the children were babies. —Grandma Freda

- Boss people around! I also like to read to them a lot. —Shana

- Everyone says I am patient, even though I do not always feel it. I also like to play games with them and support them in whatever they do. —Melody

- Give directions. —Karen

- Nurture them. My kids know I am "for them." I believe in them, even in their biggest mistakes and disappointments. —Deb

- Give my children lots of love and affirmation. —Sara

- Teach them to treat others the way they want to be treated. —Barb

- My kids know how special they are to me. I want them to know and feel this so much that even when they feel like the world has turned its back on them, they won't even question that they can turn to me. —Jenny

- I'm affectionate and truly love and enjoy our girls. I introduced them to God and kept His story before them. —Melissa

CHAPTER 4

I Want to Be a Happy Mother

My friend Sandy is so full of joy that she sparkles. I mean, literally *sparkles*. Yesterday at church she wore a sweater with tiny sequins, and in the sun her shirt shot sparkles all over the auditorium wall. She was a human disco ball, and it was a reflection of her life.

The joy Sandy has inside isn't containable; it shines right out of her. Her husband sometimes rolls his eyes at her and shakes his head, but it is clear that he is madly in love with her, even after forty years of marriage.

Do our families catch our joy like that? Do our husbands and kids enjoy being close to us because they know we are going to infect them with our joy? As mothers, we often set the emotional barometer of the house. This is why so many kitchens have signs that say, "If Mama ain't happy, ain't nobody happy," and "Happy Wife, Happy Life." This is a big responsibility we carry, and we need to train ourselves well so we can be an encouragement to our families. It's up to us to set the standard for good attitudes for our kids.

Who's in Charge Here?

It's not easy to control our emotions. We may become afraid past all reason. We may feel happy only in times of comfort and excitement. We may become angry at any small provocation. Sometimes we let anxiety rule our minds when our life circumstances change. It's not wrong to have feelings, because God hardwired them into our brains and we aren't human without them. But we can take charge of the feelings before they take charge of us.

This is so easy to say, and so hard to live! How do we actually rope in our minds? We start by examining our thoughts. Our thoughts are the fertile ground where our emotions and feelings grow. When we let ourselves dwell on negative thoughts, they are bound to give root to negative emotions. These emotions will grow so big that we can't hide them, and that's when we'll officially become That Grumpy Lady. To spare our children and other loved ones from this unpleasantness, we can train our minds to grow better thoughts. The simple truth is that we always have control over our minds and thoughts (making exception, of course, for those who face debilitating mental illness).

I'm not saying that we should have only happy thoughts so we have only joyous feelings. That's not human. We'll still have our grumpy days. The attitude problem starts when we dwell on those negative thoughts and let our view of the world turn sour.

Have you ever spent a February in Michigan? It's cold. It's dank. The wind blows, the snow dumps, and the sun rarely shines. It's awful, and it feels like it goes on *forever*. So when my husband came home from work a few months ago and casually mentioned that he'd been told about a job opening in Charleston, South Carolina, I begged him to apply. As he picked up the laptop to get the details of the job, he asked, "Why do you want to move so badly?" All I could come up with was, "I need a new life. I just need a new life." I was tired of the cold, and the house seemed too small, and I'd been staring at the back end of the neighbor's house all winter, and I had too many volunteer responsibilities, and, and, and . . .

I just wasn't happy. Not happy at all. Of course, this unhappiness wore off on my children. In fact, as I was trying to come up with a title for this book, I asked my daughter for some ideas. "Um, how about *Mommy Misery*?" she said. Ouch. Now there's a glaring example of how my emotions and attitude affect the people around me. Who wants to live with a crabby woman? Nobody! Who's in charge of determining whether I become an old grouch? I am!

As mothers, we are in control of only one person—ourselves. That's it, folks. We can't control our husbands, try as we might. We can teach our kids twenty different ways to obey, but we can't make them *want* to obey. We aren't overlord of the washing machine, the car transmission, or the principal at our kids' school. Any grasp we might have on people or things is only temporary, because eventually our hold will weaken. Instead of developing strangleholds, let's strive to control our own thoughts and feelings. Let's find a healthy balance in our own lives.

Garbage In, Garbage Out

What are you feeding your mind? We must feed our minds healthy things if we desire successful attitude management. There's no hope for true happiness if we have a mental diet of soap operas, tacky reality shows, and sordid novels. Trust me on this one, ladies, and hear me out.

I love to read mysteries and watch home shows on television. I mean, I *love* these things. But I realized a few years ago that the longer I spent watching those home improvement shows, the more depressed I got about my own circumstances. I started to deplore my small, weird kitchen and our awkward floor plan. I finally had the sense to shut off the silly TV, and my attitude started to improve a little bit at a time. It wasn't overnight, but soon I realized that my house was average for my community and I was truly blessed to have it.

The novels were harder to give up, but I'm glad I did. Now, I didn't give up secular novels altogether, but I am far more careful about my selections. This wasn't easy because I adore witty, well-written books. I would often ignore my good sense to read books that were well written, regardless of the messages they subtly directed to my mind. One of my old favorites was a series about a bounty hunter and her sidekick. The books are great fun, but I noticed a growing depression whenever I read them. I became dissatisfied with my responsibilities at home and started to long for impossibilities like moving to the East Coast alone and carrying a gun in my handbag to take down crime syndicates. Last year I took my entire, lovingly collected series and dropped it off at the library's book sale. Do I miss it? Yes, sometimes I do. But it was the best choice for my growth in Christ. The books were not encouraging me to cherish my children nor to enjoy my time as a mother.

Once we weed out the bad influences, we have to replace them with good and healthy ones. I've replaced my TV watching with studying Italian. My husband and I are planning a trip to Italy in the next few years, and we want to know enough Italian to get by comfortably. I've also searched high and wide for better novels, and I'm pleased to report that they exist. Now that my daughter is old enough to use a sewing machine without getting a needle through her finger, we've started to sew together. We're both enjoying our projects, and we're being productive. We can replace unhelpful influences with practicing soccer in the backyard, giving baking lessons, learning to rollerblade—anything! I also recommend in-depth Bible study, just for fun. You'll feel your relationship with God grow and you'll have direction in your life.

I encourage you to carefully evaluate what you are feeding your mind. Pray for God's direction. Think back carefully at any time in your life where you've had a bout of depression or anxiety, and evaluate what you had been reading or watching at that time. Is there something you're letting take root in your heart and mind that is causing you to grow in unhealthy ways? Be brave and *get rid of it!* The benefits will far outweigh the temporary loss you'll feel.

Is This a Weed or a Tulip?

Now that you're paying attention to the thoughts that run through your mind, have you noticed that not every thought is the truth? Some of that stuff is just plain crazy! Our thoughts are not infallible indicators of reality. Just like a good gardener, we must develop the ability to weed out the bad thoughts and temptations.

In the spring my little garden starts to turn green. It's a wonderful sight after a long, frozen winter. But at first, it's hard to tell what is a weed and what is a prized perennial. This spring I tore the tops off of my alliums—*again*. I did it last year, too! Their first sprouts resemble spiky grass, so I accidentally rip them out year after year. But a wise gardener would be able to determine the difference between alliums and grass. We must become the wise gardeners of our minds by finding the truth and nurturing it, while identifying the lies and uprooting them.

Second Corinthians 10:5 says, "We demolish arguments and every pretension that sets itself up against the knowledge of God, and we take captive every thought to make it obedient to Christ." Before taking something captive, we must identify whether it is friend or foe. We need to ask ourselves: "Is this thought the truth? Where did this idea come from? Is it consistent with the teachings of the Bible?" If a thought is not sound, then we need to take it captive and make it obedient to Christ by reframing it with biblical truth. For example, when my children were very small I was always exhausted and usually quite grumpy. I started to wonder if I could really be a good mother to them. I started to think that perhaps running off to a tropical paradise would be easier than getting up three times a night and changing all those dirty diapers.

No one is going to argue against early motherhood being physically exhausting, but running off to a beach house would not have solved anything. The Bible promises in Matthew 11:28–30 that God gives us the strength to accomplish the jobs He's given us, even if that job involves many dirty diapers. The Bible also promises us that Jesus is waiting for us when we are weary and overburdened. Really. He's waiting for us, wanting to help share the burden of sleepless nights and teething babies! We can't let our thoughts distract us from finding the truth and acting upon it.

We need to do this consistently, my friends. The Holy Spirit will show you when your thoughts are wrong, especially if you pray and ask Him for help in this area. Don't be deceived into thinking that every thought that comes through your mind is the truth. Test your thoughts and commit to weeding out those that don't please God. You'll be much happier when your mental garden is full of beautiful, healthy thoughts instead of lies, negativity, and selfishness.

I Could Probably Hear You If I Was Listening

Ultimately to uproot our negative thoughts and emotions, we must learn to respond to the direction of the Holy Spirit. In my experience, God is the only one who has been able to transform my mind. John 14:26 says, "The Counselor, the Holy Spirit, whom the Father will send in my name, will teach you all things and will remind you of everything I have said to you." I know that it's the Holy Spirit who reminds me to think kind thoughts when I am frustrated with my kids. He's the one who teaches me to choose my words carefully when I get crabby.

If we are going to learn from the Holy Spirit, we need to be listening, which means we need to be spending time reading the Bible and praying. It would be so much easier if the Holy Spirit just spoke audibly whenever we were about to make a huge mistake. It is rare for a person to hear God in an audible way, but our spiritual ears can still hear Him if our hearts are listening. He might speak to us with a verse that comes to mind at just the time we need it. Perhaps as we are praying the Spirit will impress something so clearly on our hearts that we know He is speaking to us.

Honestly, I've had times where I was doing *nothing* distinctly spiritual when suddenly I've felt God speak to me. Three years ago I worked briefly at a local farm that specializes in autumn activities like corn mazes and apple picking. I was at work, bent at the waist with my head in a container of pumpkins when God said to me, "Are you ready to focus on writing yet?" And let me assure you that I pulled my head out of that pumpkin crate and said, "Yes, God, I am. Get me out of here." I said that out loud, right in the middle of the pumpkin barn. I might not have been engaged in a specific spiritual activity at the moment, but this happened during a time when my prayer life had been growing stronger daily. When we make that effort to go to Him, we can be ready to hear Him when He speaks.

When we have developed a relationship with God and are listening for the Holy Spirit's prompting, He can then help us step away from the habit of reacting too quickly to every emotional trigger. He can remind us to ask God for help in discerning the proper attitude and perspective. Philippians 4:4–8 tells us to

Rejoice in the Lord always. I will say it again: Rejoice! Let your gentleness be evident to all. The Lord is near. Do not be anxious about anything, but in everything, by prayer and petition, with thanksgiving, present your requests to God. And the peace of God, which transcends all understanding, will guard your hearts and your minds in Christ Jesus. Finally, brothers, whatever is true, whatever is noble, whatever is right, whatever is pure, whatever is lovely, whatever is admirable—if anything is excellent or praiseworthy—think about such things.

This is the genuine joy that will transform us as mothers and Christians. Think of the blessing you will be to your children when your mind is full of God's joy and your thoughts are true, noble, pure, and lovely!

When you have practiced these God-honoring thought patterns, you will naturally begin to teach them to your children. Don't we also want our kids to focus on what is true, noble, right, and pure? Think of the impact you can have for God's kingdom with a sound and healthy mind that teaches others how to have the same. The ripple effect from this will affect generations after you for the good.

I have been closely watching members of the older, more mature generation of Christians, and I have something to report—it appears that this process of crucifying our sinful nature never ends. I don't think we reach a spot where we get to rest and coast on our previous holy choices. The only place we get to rest is heaven, and I know that we all have some stuff to do first. So don't give up when you make mistakes, let your emotions run amok, or start to sour your attitude. Just restart the process of praying and examining your thoughts.

The good news is that my older, mature friends have made enough good choices that they have become beautiful, calm, wonderful people. They are full of encouraging words, patient attitudes, and voices of reason. There is hope! We can grow and change, with God's help.

True Happiness

I know we want to be good mothers who bring light and blessing to their families with their happy spirits. We will develop those happy spirits only when we are able to train our minds. We can't rely on good times, easy circumstances, or the help of others to manage ourselves. True joy is a consequence of spiritual good health. When we ground ourselves in the teachings in the Bible, we will have the truth to combat the lies that enter our minds. When we pray and ask for God's wisdom and help, He will provide it for us, giving us the ultimate weapons against Satan's attacks, our culture's subtle messages, and our own selfishness and immaturity.

I encourage you to take the first steps to grow in this area. Don't be overwhelmed if the process seems too huge; just start small. Change one TV habit this week. Next week make time for reading the Bible. God will be pleased with your obedience and He will bless your efforts to know Him better. Everyone in your home will benefit from your new, true joy.

Study Questions

1. What makes you the unhappiest as a mother? Dirty diapers? Dirty house? Unending responsibilities?

2. What was the happiest moment of your life? Why?

3. Do you feel you have control over your thoughts? Can you tell the truth from a lie when it goes through your mind?

4. Please read Psalm 57. What is David feeling in this passage? What does David choose to do in the midst of his problems (see vv. 1–2, 7, 9)? How can you apply David's choices to your own life?

AREN'T YOU GLAD FOR
MEDICAL PROFESSIONALS?

I asked: Have you ever been to the emergency room with your kids? Why were you there?

Deb answered: Yes! We've been there for stitches, knocked out teeth, scarily high fevers and vomiting to the point of dehydration, and a broken finger. Then we had a serious bike injury where one of the boys hit an SUV with its tailgate down. He got a concussion, handlebars to the ribs, and a dinner-plate-sized hematoma to the thigh, and he bit through his tongue. (*Through!* We could *see* through his tongue!) And we've also been to the ER for a staple through the thumb and bleeding after eating mouse poison . . .

CHAPTER 5

I Want to Be a Healthy Mother of Healthy Kids

A few years ago my doctor ordered routine lab work with my annual physical. The results indicated unexpected and severe anemia, which launched me into several months of testing. I found myself, at age thirty-one, getting a colonoscopy. Thirty-one-year-olds should never get colonoscopies! This is something reserved for the mature generations! And while I was at the doctor's office waiting for the colonoscopy, starving, dressed in only a hospital gown, *with no coffee in my system*, the gastroenterologist looked at my chart and asked me, "Have you been tested for celiac disease?"

"No!" I practically snarled at him. I usually go out of my way to be pleasant to all health care workers. They have hard jobs and can keep me alive in precarious situations. I love doctors, but I was not happy with that one. The problem was that I had just read a book from the Mayo Clinic on all kinds of digestive disorders. I had read the book from cover to cover, twice, because the initial testing showed that I was losing blood through my digestive system. The book covered every digestive disorder imaginable. I had read the first two paragraphs of the celiac disease chapter and had thought, "Oh, how awful. I could never live with that disease!" And then I'd skipped to something more hopeful, like abdominal cancer. I am not making that up. I was not happy when the doctor suggested that I be tested for celiac. I was even less happy when my tests came back positive.

Celiac disease is an autoimmune disorder, which means that my immune system mistakenly thinks that the gluten in wheat, barley, and rye are threats, so it attacks. It attacks in the small intestine, where the gluten is being digested. Over time the small intestine becomes inflamed and leads to malnutrition, anemia, and a host of other problems. Lucky for celiacs, there is a very simple cure—stop eating gluten.

Just because the cure is simple doesn't mean it's easy. Do you know how much wheat is in American food? Bread, fried chicken, noodles, doughnuts, soy sauce, Kit Kat Bars—all of them are full of gluten. At potlucks I can never be sure of the ingredients in a dish. Eating at restaurants is dicey because the gluten can't come in contact with my food. So if the French fries are cooked in the same vat as the chicken nuggets, I can get sick because miniscule amounts of gluten have contaminated the French fries. (Please note: This often doesn't stop me from eating the French fries. This is why they invented Pepto-Bismol.) Celiacs who eat gluten deal with stomach pain, diarrhea, irritability, and fatigue. The symptoms can last for days if we eat a lot of gluten. This is not fun.

However, I'd like to report that there is an upside to the stress of the diagnosis. The symptoms of celiac disease came about so slowly that I had not noticed the downhill slide. I just felt vaguely bad all the time. When I started the iron supplements and my anemia retreated, it was like someone had given me an IV of sunshine. The gluten-free diet gave me less stomach pain in about a week, and within a few months I felt like a new woman. I had energy! I had more patience with my kids and enjoyment of my responsibilities! The diet has taken discipline and a lot of praying, but it has changed my life for the better. In fact, my relationship with God has grown because I needed Him desperately to manage the stress of the diagnosis.

I know other mothers out there are just like me. Maybe you know all too well what your health issue is, or maybe you have a general sense that all is not well. Since physical and mental health impact our abilities to be better mothers, let's look at these effects and how health influences our relationship with God.

Am I Just a Hypochondriac, or Is There Really a Problem Here?

Being sick takes a lot of energy. So does being a mother. When a body needs to heal itself and take care of other people, an energy deficit will occur. A body can do only so much. Do you find yourself dragging through your days? Do you wake up in the morning knowing you won't have enough energy to make it through the day? I've been there, my friends. Is it getting worse? *Get yourself to the doctor.* Call. Make the appointment. Tell the doctor what's going on, and he will help you! This is why he went to medical school, to help people feel well enough to make it through the day!

In my case, I was too distracted to notice that there was a problem. My health had started to deteriorate sometime after my kids were born, so I thought I was experiencing normal fatigue. After all, I was up at least once a night, and sometimes I was up several times for hours. Who wouldn't be tired? Even when I did get a whole night of sleep, I spent the day taking care of tiny people. I never considered that another problem was lurking. Let me be the warning bell for you. Think this through—are you sure something else isn't wrong? Do not hesitate to go to the doctor, look her in the eye, and say, "Listen, lady. I take three naps a day. My stomach hurts constantly and I cry all the time. I cannot do this anymore. Help me!" (Please insert your own physical and emotional issues, not mine.) She'll help you. Be brave enough to get the help you need.

Perhaps you've already been down the road of diagnosis and know exactly what your health problem is. My friend Melody and her husband have each been diagnosed with medical conditions that make them unable to have children biologically. Melody says, "It took me a while to be okay with not being able to get pregnant. But God has a plan for us and He knew that because we live so far away from family that having a baby was not an option for us." As a result, Melody and her husband have adopted two African-American boys from the foster care system, a choice that has been an enormous blessing to all members of the family.

Was this their original plan for their lives? Did they relish their health limitations? Not at all. They've had to make difficult adjustments to their expectations. But God was faithful through their difficulties, and He will be faithful to you, too.

Back to the Doctor's Office I Go

About a year and a half after I was diagnosed with celiac disease, I realized I still wasn't feeling quite right. I was nervous because I knew that autoimmune disorders sometimes cause the immune system to start attacking *everything*. Celiac disease by itself is hard enough, but if lupus, Addison's disease, or type-1 diabetes are added in, life becomes really challenging. Because my symptoms of anxiety, irritability, stomach trouble, and fatigue were growing worse again, back to the doctor I went.

During the week before the appointment, I asked God to give my doctor the wisdom to see the true problems and ask the right questions. I prayed that I would be able to clearly and concisely explain what I was feeling. Still, I was surprised when my doctor listened carefully to all of my symptoms and then gently said, "You know, these are all signs of depression." What? I was quite sure I wasn't depressed; it was just that my own body was trying to *kill me. Again.* Because she's a good doctor she ordered blood work to rule out physical problems, but she said that if the results came back normal that I should consider taking a mild dose of an antidepressant.

I agreed and took the prescription only because I knew that the lab work would show the true problem. And indeed it did—the lab work showed that I was fine in the body, which meant I needed help in the head. Begrudgingly I started the antidepressant. In a week I felt happier and more hopeful. In about a month I was going to bed at night without dreading the next day. I started to enjoy spending time with family and friends again, and my hobbies became interesting. The medicine worked well, and after a moderate treatment time of six months the doctor directed me to wean myself off the medication. I've felt fine since then.

Sometimes antidepressants are seen as a fix for weakness or for spiritual failing instead of a valid response to a health concern. I have no doubt that some people turn to antidepressants because it's easier to numb the mental pain than to make hard changes through diligent work. And some people may take antidepressants to drown out the Holy Spirit as they purposefully disobey God's principles. But there are people reading this book who pray, read the Bible, and live in obedience to God's principles and yet still struggle emotionally. If this is you, please don't let the stigma of mental health care stop you from getting the help you need. Approach the issue with prayer and accept it for what it may be—a health problem.

Counseling with a qualified professional can also work wonders. In our age, we are tremendously blessed to have a wide range of people who can help us, including psychologists, social workers, and pastors. If you are struggling, make an appointment to discuss the problem with your pastor or another church staff member. That person can help you find good options that don't cost a lot of money. Most communities have Christian and secular counselors. Remember that when a mother takes care of herself, then she will have more energy to share with her family.

Kids Need to Be Healthy, Too

As if taking care of our own health isn't a big enough challenge, as mothers we're also responsible for our kids' health. We wonder, "Does she have a regular stomachache, or the plague? Did he give himself a concussion when he fell out of the tree? Should we go to the ER, or wait until tomorrow to call the doctor? Is her arm supposed to bend that direction?" Even seemingly small health problems can feel large to a concerned mother. My friend Sara reported that one of the problems her son faced was chronic constipation. She says, "It sounds funny, but the poor baby was pooping only once a week and when he finally did go it was extremely painful for him. Finally after many changes to diet and much prayer he is functioning so much better, which is a relief (no pun intended) to all."

I'm certainly no medical professional, so this section will be brief. I just want to encourage you to consider carefully the growth, development, and health of your children. In most kids, a parent can expect to see results from their parenting efforts. For example, when you have a two-year-old you probably focus on teaching manners, obedience, and communication. And eventually, your kid gets it. By the time he turns three, you usually have a relatively well-behaved little boy. He can probably dress himself, speak complete thoughts, and obey most of the time, within his ability.

But sometimes it doesn't work out as planned. We work, and we train, and we pray, and we teach, and we discipline, and we pray some more, and we yell, and we cry. But nothing changes. At the end of the year we have a three-year-old who still screams and has tantrums and can't dress himself. Or maybe she won't talk and can't draw. Or maybe it becomes obvious that she isn't keeping up with her peers.

I have run into a few mothers who, for one reason or another, completely ignore these warning signs. They think that if they keep plugging along, everything will come out all right in the end. This strategy may cause fierce stress at home and on a marriage. Ignoring problems will not solve them. Get help to define what is ailing your child. Once you know what the need is, you can then move forward to fix the problem.

If you have concerns that something isn't right with your child, the first step is (again) prayer. *Always* pray first. God can illuminate what we never would have seen on our own, and He can fix it. But be aware that sometimes His provision comes through the help of people like teachers, doctors, counselors, psychologists, and other parents. And there are some situations that God doesn't radically improve here on earth. Just the other day I saw a family at the park with a mentally challenged, adult son. He sat on a bench and happily watched the children play. His mother was wonderful to him, treating him with kindness and respect. I don't doubt that she has days of frustration, but I could also see the peace and acceptance in her face. That peace was reflected back to her from her son. Their situation might not change, but they have peace.

In my own experience, my son Caleb had an easy first year. He was a happy, fun baby. But everything fell apart on us when he turned one. For three and a half years we tried everything we knew to do for that kid. We prayed. We disciplined. We begged. We threatened. We rewarded. Nothing. Nothing worked. One day when he was four he had a screaming fit for twenty minutes because I asked him to put on socks. Socks! A twenty-minute tantrum over socks! That was when I finally took my friend Susan's advice and scheduled an appointment with a doctor who specializes in food sensitivities. Caleb is a different kid when he's off wheat and dairy. It's almost heavenly! Sure, he still has bad days, but those days serve as reminders of where we've been and where we'd still be if we hadn't gotten him the help he needed.

If your child is struggling in an area, find the help he or she needs. There is no shame in addressing an area of concern. If your first attempt to find help doesn't work, don't stop. Find another doctor, do more research, and ask teachers for input. You might be amazed at the wisdom out there, available to help your child.

The Great Healer

Even considering all doctors can do, medical professionals will only be able to help you so much. You can only help yourself and your children so much. After humans have done their parts, you're going to need help from your loving heavenly Father, the Great Physician. As I have mentioned repeatedly, do not hesitate to pray for the doctor's wisdom, for the test results, and for your body's healing. Pray that you'll be able to communicate clearly with the medical staff so that they will understand what you need. Pray for the patience and the grace to wait for the correct diagnosis and the ability to handle that diagnosis when it comes. And pray for your adjustment as you accept the reality of your health situation and everything it requires. Pray that you'll manage to be a good mother through all of the fear, stress, and bodily strain. God will not disappoint you in this. As you reach out to Him, He will look upon you with love and mercy. He'll help you from beginning to end, if you just ask.

How do we know Jesus cares about the sick? Let's look at Luke 8:40–56. Jesus found himself in a crowd of people. A man named Jairus came and begged Jesus to heal his dying twelve-year-old daughter. Luke notes that Jairus, who was a ruler of the synagogue, fell at Jesus' feet. This man had high standing in the community, but desperation for his daughter's life brought him to Jesus without regard to the social disapproval it would bring. Jesus' teaching made the Jewish religious leaders defensive and nervous, which led to an uneasy relationship between them. Jairus' colleagues would not have approved of him seeking out Jesus for help. But Jairus didn't care; his daughter was dying and this traveling teacher was rumored to have healing abilities.

Jesus, already loving this family and wanting to ease their pain, was on the way to their home when a woman snuck up behind him in the pressing crowd and grabbed the edge of His coat. She was instantly healed of bleeding that no professional had been able to fix in twelve years. Jesus turned around, lovingly told her that her faith had made her well, and then went on His way to get the twelve-year-old girl back on her feet. The girl had died while her father had been out hunting for Jesus, but this didn't stop Jesus at all. He took her by the hand and revived her.

Really get into this picture with me, please. Imagine yourself in these situations. What would it take for *you* to drop to Jesus' feet in front of a crowd, knowing full well that your job and your social status were on the line? Or, can you imagine yourself sneaking up behind a man to grab the hem of his dusty coat while a tight crowd pressed up against you?

I don't know that Jairus or this woman were any different from us. Jairus probably wasn't comfortable making a spectacle of himself or begging for help from a busy man.

And the woman sought a stealthy healing—she only revealed herself when Jesus turned around to ask who touched Him. Something within each of them drove them to Jesus in their crisis. Somehow they knew He could heal and make all well. This is the God we serve. Jesus had full power to heal a woman and bring a girl back to life in the same afternoon. What's more, He *wanted* to heal them. He wanted them to come in their desperation and pain. He wanted to touch them lovingly and bless them. And He wants us to come to Him when we need His healing touch.

Claim this passage of Scripture for yourself if you are struggling with your health. This problem won't consume you or put you in a place where God cannot help you. I'm not going to give false hope—you or your child may not be healed in the way you wish. You might have to deal with this for the rest of your days. But God's Word teaches that if we hope in Him and seek Him, He will comfort us. Second Corinthians 1:3–4 says, "Praise be to the God and Father of our Lord Jesus Christ, the Father of compassion and the God of all comfort, who comforts us in all our troubles." Even if we do not receive instantaneous relief, we can be assured that Jesus is still able to bring comfort to any circumstance.

How Are You Feeling Today?

A family functions best when everyone is healthy physically, mentally, and emotionally. As mothers we must do our best for our children and ourselves, and we must never be afraid to look to outside help when a situation is beyond us. God, our doctors, and our friends and family will help us if we ask. I hope you are involved in a loving church that can encourage you and support you as well.

In addition, we may need to be the helpers. If you know of a family that is suffering, don't be afraid to speak up *gently and lovingly*. We must be careful that our well-intended words do not come across as judgmental and rude. If you're uncertain on how to proceed, pray first. Then wait patiently for an opening when the problem is obvious and very, very carefully choose your words. You may be the link to a family finding the physical, mental, or emotional stability it needs.

May God grant you and your loved ones health! I know He's ready to help anytime we ask, so don't hesitate to search for His blessing. You may be surprised at the solution and at how soon you're back to your spritely old self.

Study Questions

1. Are you feeling well today?
2. When was the last time you had a physical?
3. Do you feel healthy mentally? Are you receiving good care if this is a struggle for you?
4. Are there areas of your children's health or development that concern you? Are they keeping up reasonably well with their peers? Is your family life functioning smoothly? If not, do you know where you can find help?
5. For further study, read Isaiah 38:14–19; Lamentations 3:19–26; 2 Corinthians 12:7–10; Revelation 21:3–4.

OH, FOR CRYING OUT LOUD

I asked: What has changed about your appearance since you became a mother?

Jenny answered: I've been known to walk through the grocery store with my shirt covered in spit up and not notice it.

CHAPTER 6

I Want to Be a Pretty Mother, Surrounded by Pretty Things

When I was a child Isaiah 52:7 cracked me up. It reads, "How beautiful on the mountains are the feet of those who bring good news, who proclaim peace, who bring good tidings, who proclaim salvation, who say to Zion, 'Your God reigns!'" It's a zany thought, those beautiful feet on the mountain. But it made some sense to me. I loved my feet. They're nice feet. They get me where I need to go and look nice in sandals.

As an adult, I understand that Isaiah wrote about beautiful feet because messengers used to run from battles to people who were anxiously waiting for news. The citizens wondered, "Are we winning? Is everyone okay? Are we about to be taken captive as slaves?" Good news brought joy to the people. And isn't that a key part of beauty? True beauty brings good to others.

I've worked hard on my yard and house to make them welcoming and comfortable to visitors. I've ripped out ugly bushes and planted beautiful flowers, torn down appalling wallpaper and repainted with fresh colors. Eric and I have gutted the bathroom and put new flooring throughout the whole house. My husband thought I was crazy, but this was a deep need in my soul—I hated to be surrounded by hideousness. And let me tell you, the wallpaper in my living room was nothing short of hideous.

Most mothers understand. As women, we love pretty things. Admittedly, some women are practical to their core and some men love beautiful surroundings and nice clothes. But by and large, we women have the market cornered on loveliness. I think this is the way God created us, and we should embrace the desire to make ourselves and our surroundings pretty. However, as with any desire, it can get out of control. It can lead to idolizing ourselves, youth, and earthly beauty.

Those beautiful messengers in Isaiah brought words of life: good news, peace, good tidings, salvation, and the message that "Your God reigns!" In the same way, beautiful people offer words of life to others. Are we full of good news and good tidings? Do we have a message of peace and salvation? Good things come out of our mouths only when good and beautiful things are inside our hearts.

Let's face it; beautiful objects are not a real need for motherhood. Patience is a need. Kindness is a need. But I can look like death warmed over in the ugliest house in America and still be a great mother. Even so, this subject is important to motherhood. Our daughters and sons are watching how we approach this subject, and our attitude will affect them.

We can find a healthy balance in beauty as we seek God's perspective in His Word. Once we have learned God's heart on the matter, then we can move forward to apply it to our lives and teach our children. With that in mind, we'll first discuss the biblical perspective of beauty and then apply it to parenting.

Such a Challenging Passage

Peter authored a little section of Scripture that has been a big challenge to Christ-followers for hundreds of years. He wrote this portion directly to wives, and the message is not easy. Under the direction of the Holy Spirit, Peter wrote,

> Wives, in the same way be submissive to your husbands so that, if any of them do not believe the word, they may be won over without words by the behavior of their wives, when they see the purity and reverence of your lives. Your beauty should not come from outward adornment, such as braided hair and the wearing of gold jewelry and fine clothes. Instead, it should be that of your inner self, the unfading beauty of a gentle and quiet spirit, which is of great worth in God's sight. For this is the way the holy women of the past who put their hope in God used to make themselves beautiful. They were submissive to their own husbands, like Sarah, who obeyed Abraham and called him her master. You are her daughters if you do what is right and do not give way to fear. (1 Peter 3:1–6)

Entire books have been written on this passage, and I'm not going to try to re-create them here. Let's just agree that the topic of submission is foreign to our modern culture and hard to apply to our daily lives. We'll set the discussion aside while we focus on the subject of true beauty. This passage has some of the most direct teaching the Bible has to offer on the subject.

First, Peter encourages us to develop lives of such purity and reverence that we can win our husbands (and other people) without words. We ladies are experts at winning people over without words, but we've been taught to show some skin, shorten the skirt, and push up the bosom to do it. You know what I'm talking about. A woman dressed in this way walks into a meeting and every man in the room becomes deeply interested in whatever she has to say. However, God holds us to a higher standard. People will be attracted to us when purity and reverence define our hearts. This means that our motives reflect our desire to love others as God intended.

Second, Peter teaches us that beauty and decorations are two different things, not to be confused with one another. Earrings are decoration. Fancy hairstyles are decoration. But true beauty will be found in a quiet and gentle spirit. Frankly, putting in earrings would be so much easier than the work involved in developing a quiet and gentle spirit. But again, God is holding us as His children to a higher standard. A quiet and gentle spirit is calm, trusting, and thoughtful of others. These attributes are gorgeous on any woman and will never fade, wrinkle, or sag. Our heavenly Father values them highly.

As mothers, this is exactly what we need to teach our children. All the flash and sparkle of our culture will fade away. The fancy clothes, the trendy accessories, and the truly fabulous shoes mean nothing if we don't work to develop the right things in our hearts.

A Beautiful Offering

A story about a woman with a beautiful heart is recorded in Matthew 26:6–13. It reads,

> While Jesus was in Bethany in the home of a man known as Simon the Leper, a woman came to him with an alabaster jar of very expensive perfume, which she poured on his head as he was reclining at the table. When the disciples saw this, they were indignant. "Why this waste?" they asked. "This perfume could have been sold at a high price and the money given to the poor." Aware of this, Jesus said to them, "Why are you bothering this woman? She has done a beautiful thing to me. The poor you will always have with you, but you will not always have me. When she poured this perfume on my body, she did it to prepare me for burial. I tell you the truth, wherever this gospel is preached throughout the world, what she has done will also be told, in memory of her."

Now, imagine this scene with me. Let's pretend you had a male friend, and he was hanging out after dinner with a group of his friends. What would motivate you to walk into that room and pour an offering of perfume on his head? When I imagine this scene with people from my own life, the emotions and actions stand out even more clearly. I like my preacher a lot, but if he was chatting with the elders I wouldn't walk in the room and pour perfume all over his head. I might knock and quietly offer everyone coffee or donuts, but I have never been moved to this woman's level of emotion in public. The public nature of this woman's gift really affects me.

It must have been an intense moment, and some of the disciples (primarily Judas, who was stealing from the common purse) got angry with her and rebuked her for the perceived waste. But Jesus saw the whole thing differently, and it's always Jesus' perspective that we must seek. He told the disciples to leave her alone. Can you imagine the rush of pure love the woman must have felt when Jesus defended her actions? When she realized that He understood her intentions and her gift?

Jesus thought the gift was *beautiful*. Why? I'm sure the perfume smelled lovely, but it would have worn off eventually. I think it was beautiful because it was the most precious symbol she could find to show Jesus how much He meant to her and how committed she was to Him. Jesus saw the gift as an offering that reflected the deep love in her heart, and He was moved by the beauty of it.

What do we have to offer Jesus? What can we give Him that is so beautiful it will move Him to our defense in the middle of an angry world? We have nothing, unless we have taken our heart, confessed the filth, and turned it over to our Lord in devotion. Then we can offer to Jesus the songs He has gifted us to sing, the bathtub we have scrubbed to brilliance for our family, the books He has allowed us to write, or the children that we lovingly train for His kingdom. The gifts are made beautiful because of the beautiful heart that offers them.

It Doesn't Get Much Uglier than a Dirty Grave

One caution—we can't fake beauty and hope God doesn't notice. Jesus spoke pointedly about the problem caused when a beautiful exterior doesn't have an internal beauty to accompany it. In Matthew 23:27–28, Jesus spoke to the Pharisees and teachers of the law, men who were widely respected as Israel's moral, religious, and ethical leaders. They knew the laws and kept the commandments, but their hearts were far from God. From the outside they were holy and attractive, but Jesus saw straight through their façades to the ugliness they hid in their hearts. He said to them,

> "Woe to you, teachers of the law and Pharisees, you hypocrites! You are like whitewashed tombs, which look beautiful on the outside but on the inside are full of dead men's bones and everything unclean. In the same way, on the outside you appear to people as righteous but on the inside you are full of hypocrisy and wickedness."

That's a strong rebuke! Jesus was *not happy* with the men who presented themselves as attractive and holy while disregarding their hearts.

Ladies, we must apply this teaching to ourselves. Like the Pharisees, we are the moral and ethical examples in our homes. A few years ago, when I could still eat wheat, my daughter came to me and asked for more Oreos. I told her no, because the two of us had eaten too many Oreos already and we both knew it. Suddenly, like a flash of lightning, I realized (or more accurately, the Holy Spirit convicted me) that I was planning on having more Oreos as soon as her back was turned. I was teaching her discipline in her eating habits that I was disregarding myself. My name is Jessie, and I am a hypocrite.

That moment was a turning point in my life. I realized that I had to learn the lesson myself, and *then* I had the right to teach it to my children. We need beautiful hearts before we can expect to help our children develop them. If the kids are defiant and surly, we have to ask ourselves whether they are learning that from us. If they are rude and thoughtless, we have to consider how we treat them (or others). The beauty must begin in our clean, humble, and God-honoring hearts. Then we pray the kids will learn it from us.

My Bod Is Beau-tee-ful

My son was a somewhat enormous baby. He weighed nine pounds and three ounces and was nine days overdue. Let me assure you that my stomach will never look the same again. I now have one particular stretch mark (among the many others) that creates a wrinkly split at the top of my belly button. It's not my favorite thing, and sometimes I bemoan its existence. Those of you who have had twins are thinking, "Lady, you don't know what a stretched-out belly is until you've squeezed *two* babies in there." And what the pregnancies don't damage, time does. We're all headed for the same little old lady look, my friends. We might as well accept that fate and move on. To flabby upper arms, a round belly, and knobby knuckles—I welcome you.

Okay, *welcome* is a strong word. "I accept you" might be more accurate. This acceptance will be possible only if my heart has been focused on the right things all along. The time is now, ladies. Let's not spend the next thirty years pursuing cute boots and cardio programs, only to find ourselves in retirement realizing that we have no depth to our souls, no true relationship with God, *and* no cute body to coast us through our remaining years.

This is not to say that we shouldn't spend some time spiffing up the old body. I don't think God wants us to run around with a heart full of His grace and truth but dressed in polyester leisure suits we inherited when Great-Aunt Annie died ten years ago. It's certainly not wrong to have a nice hairstyle and clothes that make us feel good. Fabulous and fun clothes are a perk of being a woman. Remember, our appearance to the outside world should reflect God's work in our hearts. This includes the words we say, the attitudes we display, and even our physical appearance. God is doing something beautiful inside, so we shouldn't be afraid to look beautiful on the outside. We just have to make sure that our priorities are right.

Our kids are watching what we *do* and mostly ignoring what we *say* in this area. We're teaching without words. If we worship our bodies and neglect our souls, they will notice. If we neglect our bodies and appearance, they will see that too. All the preaching and nagging in the world won't overcome the example that we set for them each day. So let's show them how we read God's Word and pray. Let's show them how we serve at church. Then they can see us exercise, pick our clothes carefully, paint our nails, and try on three different pairs of shoes before we leave for work. We can talk about the subject only after we've set a good example.

My House and Myself: The Never-Ending Problem

I have a problem. I love houses, and I love them a lot. I like to redecorate them, repaint them, and remodel them. I like them freshly built, old as the hills, and everywhere in between. It doesn't matter how beautiful a room is because I will mentally redecorate it; I cannot stop myself. I don't spend much time in the woods or mountains because there aren't enough houses to look at. Who needs three hundred acres of trees when we could put houses in there? You see how I have a problem.

The problem is that this love of mine isn't exactly supported by Scripture. The Bible has plenty to say about buildings, foundations, and carpentry. There are even entire chapters about Solomon's temple and its furnishings (2 Chronicles 2–4). It was a glitzy place, but that was because God himself was going to reside there. This is an altogether different proposition than our decorating plans. God doesn't teach us to idolize our homes any more than He advocates idolizing any other possessions.

Our houses are tools. Just like the hammer and the garden hose, we are to use them as a means to an end; they are not the end in themselves. Our homes shelter us, give us a place to gather together, and store the few items we need to make life comfortable. We're also to use them for the ministry of hospitality, which is the act of reaching out to others to make them comfortable and welcome in our home.

A ministry of hospitality extends to a wide range of people. First, our own family needs to feel welcome in the home. A few years ago I was daily irritated because the house was always messy. Not dirty, messy. Books spilled out of the shelves. Markers poked out from under the couch. I spent too much time picking up toys. And while I cleaned I muttered, quietly at first and then louder. Finally I realized that I was making our home uncomfortable for my family. A grumpy woman who marches about cleaning up after everybody is just not a nice thing to have in a home.

So I stopped. I stopped having a bad attitude and I lowered my expectations. I now aim for "community standards of safety and decency" instead of "magazine photo shoot perfection." This means that I walk through my house and avert my eyes from small things that are out of place. With practice it's easier than I expected. Now I can (almost) greet unexpected guests without apologizing for the house. This was not a possibility under the old Clean Regime.

Also, I calmly explained to the children that any mess they left behind would be gathered, without warning, and thrown into a special bin. As the mother, I am in charge of the bin and would allow the contents to be retrieved with special chores. Very big, very ugly special chores. It's worked like a charm, I'm pleased to say. I haven't even had to buy the bin; the kids are convinced that I mean it and are learning to pick up their stuff. Our home has become comfortable again for everyone who lives in it.

Second, we are called to be hospitable to guests. This includes adults, of course, but also our children's friends. How we treat those friends means a great deal to our kids. It will also mean a lot to the children who visit. Just think—we may be the only Christians these children know. What an amazing gift to invite them into our homes and show them how Christ changes a family.

In order for the kids to feel comfortable, we need to strike a balance between too clean and too messy. No one is comfortable in a dirty, disorganized, neglected house. But we can't have such high standards that the visiting kids are terrified to break something, dirty something, or offend us. I recommend that we get the house in decent order, open the doors, take a deep breath, and let the good times roll. The carpet can be vacuumed later. The deck can be hosed down from all the Popsicle drippings. The gum will probably come out of the dog's fur. Just focus on welcoming the young ones and teaching them that God loves them and we love them too.

Reflecting the Source

It's obvious that our God values beauty. His creation is filled with color and drama. The stars sparkle at night. The mountains soar into snowy peaks. The water radiates with the glow of the sun. It's all so *gorgeous*.

There's no shame in being a part of that beauty, of reflecting God's gorgeousness to the world around us. But we need to remember that the source of that beauty must always be God working in our hearts. When we desire to give good things to others, be it our words, gifts, appearance, or home, we will be showing true beauty as God intends. Others will be attracted to us because they see God working in us and want to see more of Him.

Our children will benefit when we have a sincere heart and desire to reflect God. They will learn from our example, and one day we hope that they will have their own ministry of beauty. Let's give them the tools to make that a real possibility.

Study Questions

1. How many pairs of fashionable jeans do you own? After reading this chapter, do you feel that number is too high? Too low? Just right?

2. What was your mother's attitude about beauty? How has it affected your adult life? Do you want to pass on your inherited views to your children?

3. How much time do you spend doing your hair every day? How much time do you spend reading the Bible?

4. What would happen if you let a passel of six-year-old boys into your home for a whole afternoon? Could you survive? Welcome them? Enjoy the experience?

5. For further study, read Psalm 27:4; Ecclesiastes 3:11; Isaiah 53:2–5.

WHY IS THAT KID WEARING HIS SISTER'S PANTS?

I asked: How do you set your priorities each day? How do you decide what has to be done and what can slide?

Shana answered: Usually I prioritize by what is annoying me the most. I don't go to bed very often without having most tasks done. Things like dusting the baseboards or scrubbing the tub slide if no one complains about them. But I don't let something go if someone could potentially get sick from it, or if someone would be naked because of it.

As stressed out and anxious as I may get about my day, God always gives me the time and energy to do everything my family requires. It is not my strength, or my diligence, or some amazing skill I have acquired. As long as I don't give up ("faint not," Paul wrote), I can lie down at night and find reward in the day.

IF I'M NOT INVOLVED, THE WORLD WILL SURELY COLLAPSE

I asked: Were you ever discontent with your life, as a mother or in general?

Barb answered: I was discontent a lot when I was younger and I really wish I had not been and that I had enjoyed life more. I think it was connected to feeling so responsible, like I bore the weight of the world on my shoulders. I needed to experience God's grace! I also compared myself a lot to people who were godly, or who I thought were godly. I would try to incorporate their particular characteristics or adapt their lifestyle and be discontent when I did not measure up to them in my mind.

CHAPTER 7

I Want to Be
a Productive Mother

I have a friend with boundless energy. I think. There's a good chance that she's either faking it and sleepwalking through her days, or manic. She and her husband have six children, ages four through eighteen. Deb and Peter homeschool the oldest five kids with a devotion that I cannot even fathom. The oldest boys just took courses in Latin, for crying out loud. Deb often bakes five loaves of whole wheat bread at a time after grinding wheat in her own mill. She'll post on Facebook about how the whole family is outdoors, staining the deck and pulling out shrubs so they can plant flowers.

She makes me tired. I try not to think too much about this, or it gets me in a funk. Mind you, I'm not a total slouch myself. My house is mostly clean and organized, my husband comes home to a healthy and hot dinner (usually), and my kids are relatively well behaved and educated. I have a flower garden in the front and a vegetable garden in the back that I disallow the tallest weeds from overtaking. And that's good enough for the four of us. The end.

How do you rate yourself on the "Productive Mother" scale? Did you even know there was such a thing? There really isn't; I just made it up. Yet, we all know the scale follows us around all day, measuring what we have accomplished against the tasks yet untouched.

Now *you're* trying not to think about it, lest you fall into your own funk.

Our energy takes us only so far each day. We might have the strength to do five duties really well, but we're faced with thirty tasks to manage, direct, complete, and finagle. So we compromise and do fifteen tasks halfway. Then we rarely have important jobs done as well as we'd like, and the unfinished work ends up as clutter. My mother admitted, "Generally I don't accomplish all I set out to do. Years ago, frustrated with what I didn't get done, I made a list of all the things I *did* get done. It was amazing how much was listed."

Have you tried this? Right now, write a list of everything you have accomplished today, or this week. If you have a tiny baby, the one thing on your list may be "I kept this kid alive and mostly clean." That's good enough; we understand. The rest of us will probably have accomplished dozens of tasks that we hadn't even considered.

Now look closely at your list. Whether we're ready to acknowledge it or not, the items on our lists reflect our recent priorities. If we don't set our priorities, they will be set for us. Minute by minute, our time will be frittered away on unimportant things. How many times have we sat down next to our child to talk, but then became distracted for an hour by Facebook? Or perhaps we meant to take the kids to the park, but find ourselves reorganizing the basement while the kids wait for us on the steps. We have to wrestle our priorities back from the multitude of distractions that can snatch them away.

Resetting Our Priorities

Now that we've created a list to learn how we really spend our time, let's make a list of how we wish we spent our time. What do you *want* your priorities to be? Perhaps we aim to be attentive mothers who play with the kids a lot, or teach them to read. Maybe we want to teach Sunday school or lead the local Scouts troop. A few of us may have listed "cook organic dinners for family nightly" or "volunteer at school twenty hours a week." When we compare our ideal priority list with our reality list, does anything match? Are we setting and maintaining our own priorities? What we do is a good indication of our actual beliefs. We may tell ourselves that we put our families first, but perhaps our lists have revealed that we don't.

Have you discovered areas that require adjustments? Ladies, I call you to set priorities and stick to them! Until recently I didn't know I could set priorities and politely refuse any other requests. I thought I had to say yes to every need that crossed my path. So I did say yes, and we all suffered for it. Let me be the one to tell you that we don't have to live this way!

Two books helped me see my struggles in this area, *Becoming a Woman of Simplicity* by Cynthia Heald and *A Woman After God's Own Heart* by Elizabeth George. These women both speak from decades of service to God's kingdom. They encourage Christians to start each day with Bible study and prayer, and by asking God to set the priorities and schedule. After that they recommend focusing on family needs, and then work, church, and community. God will direct us and set our priorities if we ask. We may politely decline whatever doesn't fit within His directions.

When I realized this, a burden rolled off my shoulders! I was trying to do too much, and some of it I wasn't even that good at. I was just convinced I had to meet every need out there. After praying and resetting my priorities I went through a month where I quit almost everything. I quit volunteering at the library and school, I quit bookkeeping for my friends, and I quit the Wednesday night class at church. I did not quit teaching the first-through-third grade Sunday school class or trustee work at church because they fit well with my passions, abilities, and available time. Both of my children are in that Sunday school class, and I just really enjoy being a trustee. After the activities purge, I'm glad to report that I'm in a much better mood and I have the time and energy for God's priorities for my life—prayer and Bible reading, my husband, my kids, and friends who need me.

Some of the activities I quit I know I will add back in. For example, I am not called to homeschool my children, but I know I need to be involved in their schooling. So I will be back in their classrooms this fall. Resetting priorities doesn't mean I get more hours to nap each day; it means I get more hours to do a few important jobs really well.

I Have Family Time Scheduled Today

We touched on this in the chapter on health—kids take a lot of energy to mother well. They have a lot of energy themselves, and it can be hard to keep up with the chaos that can surround them. They come into this world knowing nothing and needing everything, and as a mother you are the primary person to teach them what they need to know. And even though our husbands are fully functional adults, they still need our attention too. They appreciate warm food and peaceful homes and we're usually the ones who make this happen.

This wouldn't be such a challenge if the world wasn't breathing down our neck, demanding our time and energy too. Many of us have jobs outside the home that cannot be ignored. My friend Sandy told me that because she worked from 8:00 a.m. to 5:00 p.m. when her son was young, she kept a firm weekly schedule for her family. She and her husband reserved Saturday mornings for laundry and cleaning, Sundays for church and friends, and weeknights for fixing dinner and spending time with their son. Her schedule didn't allow for a lot of flexibility, but it did allow her priorities to be just that—priorities. We also have responsibilities to our parents, extended family, and friends. Many of us have volunteer positions in our church and community. It's all important, and we don't want to neglect these duties.

Recently on the TLC show *19 Kids and Counting*, the Duggar parents were working on the revisions of a new book. These lovely Christian people have nineteen biological children whom they are faithfully raising for God. As Michelle and Jim Bob sat at the dining room table, they were interrupted many, many times. One of the interviewers asked Michelle how she gets anything done on the book with all the interruptions. She just laughed and gently replied that the *kids* are her work. They are her priority. The book is the interruption. Michelle has set her family as her priority, and the rest of the world falls in around that. The book will probably take three times longer for her and Jim Bob to complete than it would for a writer without nineteen children. But this isn't bothering her any, as her priority from God is being managed beautifully.

If our husband and children are our priorities, how do we work that out in real life? I think the answer is different for each family. In chapter 3 I mentioned how much I needed to work outside the home. I'm going to be honest: I would have been happy to work full-time. But as Eric and I sat down to set our priorities, a limit of ten hours each week became the obvious decision. At that time Eric worked the afternoon shift and was able to stay home with the kids while I worked. We figured out how to make our marriage and kids a priority while I got a little break and added to the family income. We found a solution that worked for our family.

Your family faces a unique set of circumstances. To assess your situation, first pray to ask God for His wisdom and perspective on your priorities. You do not want to do this with your own wisdom and perspective; you're too involved to think clearly. Then make a list of all the things you do in a month that take your energy away from your family. Which are absolutely necessary? What can change? Think broadly and carefully, and do not make an impulsive decision that will add more stress.

There's a tiny story in three of the gospels about Jesus spending time with children. Matthew, Mark, and Luke each record this moment in just two or three verses (Matthew 19:13–15; Mark 10:13–16; Luke 18:15–17). It's wedged between Jesus' teaching the crowds and the Pharisees, and the story of a rich young man. In short, Jesus' ministry was rolling full steam ahead and also attracting powerful people.

He was convicting the sinners, finding the lost, healing the broken, and teaching the untaught. He was busy. And He wasn't busy doing random work; He was doing the very work of God.

In the middle of this, parents were realizing that Jesus had supernatural power and they wanted it to touch their children. I'm not convinced that every parent there understood that Jesus was the Son of God, but they knew He had some sort of ability to bless and heal. Ancient Jewish parents were no less anxiety-stricken and panicked than we are, and they wanted something that would protect and provide for their kids. So these people wanted to plop their kids on Jesus' lap.

The disciples, anxious to get on with important business, were irritated at this interruption of children. Children! They weren't in the schedule. They didn't have any sway in the government or at the temple. They might spit up on the Messiah, and where would they have found a fresh tunic for Him? In their irritation, the disciples rebuked the parents. They felt that they knew what was best for Jesus' schedule and they weren't going to allow these interlopers to mess up the plan.

Ah, but they had forgotten to consult the Messiah. They were focused on their plan, not the point. Mark 10:14–16 says that Jesus was indignant. He said to His disciples, "Let the little children come to me, and do not hinder them, for the kingdom of God belongs to such as these. I tell you the truth, anyone who will not receive the kingdom of God like a little child will never enter it." Then he took the children in his arms, put his hands on them, and blessed them. Jesus wasn't on board with the disciples' plan. His priorities always aligned with His heavenly Father's plan, and that clearly involved blessing the children with His time and loving touch.

Are we offering the same blessings to our children and husbands? Do they see that we will stop the freight train of our daily schedule to bless them with what they need? I pray that God will show you what your priorities need to be for your family today, and that you will act on them with obedience.

Reaching Beyond These Walls

After we have made a careful appraisal of our family's needs, we will probably still have time and energy remaining for a project or two that God will give us in our community or church body. There are some seasons of life where this just isn't possible, I know. My friend Jenny has a six-day-old baby and two older daughters, and that is all the fun that woman can handle right now. Providing clean clothes and food and keeping the five people in her house emotionally sound is all she has on her agenda each day. Some of you may be caring for elderly parents or children with profound disabilities. It's okay if God tells you that is your one thing to do. Do it well and let the rest of the world handle itself for a while.

The rest of us need to be active in our church and community, even though we don't let those responsibilities take away from our family and sap us of all energy. Once again, pray for God's direction. Where can you best serve with the talents He has given you? Every community has thousands of needs and you can't meet them all. In my own small church I could serve in almost fifteen different areas, from teaching Sunday school to mowing the enormous lawn, from balancing the checkbook to scrubbing the potties. My husband and

I both serve in two areas and sometimes that's more than we can comfortably handle. There's no way we can add more to the load without going under. The needs still exist, but we aren't the ones to meet them.

Once you have carefully identified your priorities, you'll be ready to find the right place to serve. Know your strengths and choose well. If you do this, you will find a balance between personal, family, and community needs. The Lord will lead you if you ask Him to do so.

God's Plan Is the Only Priority

When we sort through the muddle we have created in our own lives, we'll see that we've filled our space with a lot of clutter. I mean this physically—where but in the U.S. could we throw out two-thirds of our possessions and still have enough? But more importantly, I mean this emotionally and spiritually. We allow distractions into our lives that take away from what is most important. We allow our perspective of what's important to cloud God's plan and direction. It doesn't matter how much energy we have each day if we aren't directing it to what God wants.

When I told you to pray carefully about your priorities in the above sections, what I really meant was that you should throw your own priorities right out and start fresh with God's direction. I can think of few sadder situations than lives wasted on the wrong things. God can and will get our attention and redirect us, and let this book be that attention grabber if you need it. Don't let the rest of your life slide away as you spend your energy on nothing important. Understanding the message here and now will be a lot less frightening than the other ways God can get our attention.

Speaking of which, let's talk about Saul from the New Testament. That man had energy. He had motivation. He was on the move to protect God and the religion he had been taught. He had official permission to act and he took his responsibility very, very seriously. These verses from Acts show Saul's fervor:

- He watched a mob stone Stephen after preaching Christ's truth (7:58).

- He not only watched the stoning; he approved of it (8:1).

- He actively attempted to destroy the church (8:3).

- He went from home to home, looking for Christ followers (8:3).

- When he found a believer, he dragged him or her off to prison. Gender made no difference (8:3).

- He so hated the church that he breathed out murderous threats against the disciples (9:1).

- He went to the high priest seeking a letter so that he could officially drag Christ followers from Damascus to Jerusalem. He wasn't satisfied with getting the Christians in one city; he wanted to branch out his efforts (9:2).

Saul probably never acted halfheartedly. If his mind was engaged in a project, his whole person followed suit. Let's remember that Saul really thought he was doing the right thing. His motivation was to protect what he believed were the ways of God.

But God disagreed with him and stopped him cold by blinding him on the road to Damascus. In full view of

Saul's friends and cohorts, God put him on his knees. While blinded, Saul grasped the truth that Jesus was in fact the Messiah and God's Son. Once his foundational thinking shifted, he then redirected all of his energy. He obeyed God with every fiber of his being, no matter what the cost.

The costs were huge. Saul lost his social standing, his religious friends, and probably his family's approval. His zeal for the Lord was so great I wonder if he even noticed. The Bible says that he spent three days blinded in Damascus before God sent a disciple named Ananias to place his hands upon Saul to restore his sight. Saul was baptized immediately and spent several days with the Christians in Damascus. Acts 9:20 says, "At once he began to preach in the synagogues that Jesus is the Son of God." The guy took a few days to get his bearings and off he went, preaching a new message to his former colleagues and cronies. "After many days had gone by, the Jews conspired to kill him" (Acts 9:23). He whipped up such a spiritual storm that his former allies wanted him dead. Now that's energy, my friends.

Anybody can get excited about something for a short time, but Saul never lost that fervor for teaching the truth of Christ. He wanted everyone to know Jesus and the new life He offers. Without regard to his personal well-being, Paul (as he was eventually known) served Christ until his death. Second Corinthians 11:23–29 reports that Paul suffered greatly during his years of evangelism, from imprisonment, beatings, stoning, shipwrecks, danger, overwork, poverty, thirst, lack of sleep, cold, lack of sufficient clothing, and constant emotional strain for the churches and new believers he served.

I am not asking you, and God probably isn't either, to survive a shipwreck to prove your devotion to God's priorities.

But we have to ask ourselves, do we have that kind of commitment? Have we looked to God for His direction and then thrown ourselves wholeheartedly into the project? Often we get all fired up after a sermon on Sunday and then forget the point somewhere between the church parking lot and whatever restaurant we choose for lunch. Our daily life drowns out God's priorities, overwhelming them with daily concerns like lawns that need to be mowed, clothes that need to be folded, and shows that need to be watched. In the muck of our lives, we forget one of the most basic and important commands we have—to love one another.

Have we reached out to the neighbors today? We don't need to get shipwrecked in order to follow that command. Have we spoken gently to our husbands, the clumsy cashier, and our in-laws? Have we put their needs before our own? We don't need to spend two years in prison to make God's priorities part of our daily lives. Even if we're sort of vague on the big plans God has for us, we can always, always follow through on the commands to love God and others.

If the Holy Spirit has been prompting you about your priorities for a while and you have been ignoring Him, don't hesitate to obey Him now. Act in obedience as soon as you can. God works through humble, obedient hearts. If you reset your priorities, you will give God the opportunity to work wonders in your life.

Streamlined and Making Progress

I hope I've encouraged you to action, not further depleted what little energy you had at the start of this chapter. I know it can be hard to separate from some of the responsibilities and fun. We feel guilty whenever our actions, like quitting, affect others. But let me leave you with one thought—if something is truly a priority, then the effort it requires will be worth it.

There may be days when the sacrifice feels too deep, like some of the very long days I had at home with two tiny children. It was so hard, but it was worth it. I don't regret our attempt to prioritize our family over income, even though being a full-time stay-at-home mom wasn't a workable long-term solution for our family. Eric and I had to tweak our approach to finding God's best for our family. We had to find a way to balance our children's needs, my emotional stability, and our finances, so adding a small part-time job was a good change. Don't be discouraged if you also need to adjust your choices as you follow God. He is looking for obedient, willing hearts, not perfect performance.

I believe that all families will benefit when we choose God's priorities. You will never regret the time you spent with your children. You will never regret the efforts you made to make your husband's life more enjoyable. Because this is a way that we fulfill Jesus' most basic command to love one another. God's priorities are never too burdensome if we work together with Him on the project. I encourage you to find His plan and perspective and apply them faithfully to your daily life.

Study Questions

Let's take a few minutes to study that ancient Woman of Energy, the woman outlined in Proverbs 31. I need to be honest. This woman overwhelms me. To save you from the same fate, I implore you not to impose all of these responsibilities upon yourself right away. Let's just see her as a woman who faithfully served God and her family to the best of her ability. Because, frankly, none of us have the energy to make breakfast for the servant girls before the sun rises. With that in mind, read Proverbs 31:10–31 and answer the following questions.

1. Where are her children mentioned? What does she do for them?
2. What does she do for her husband?
3. How does she help the family's income?
4. How does she reach out to the community?
5. What are her priorities?
6. How does she love the people around her?
7. What part of this life mimics your own?
8. What can you learn and apply from this example?

AN INTERVIEW WITH MY FRIEND DEB

Deb and I share the same love for God and deep desires to be the best mothers we can be, but our families look very different. She and her husband have six children; the oldest is nearly eighteen and the youngest is four. Deb and Peter homeschool the oldest five children with excellence. These parents made their family a clear priority, which has required sacrifice and intentional, difficult choices. But even with the challenges, their family is full of joy and fun and I'm so glad I can call them my friends. I asked Deb to provide input on the choices she and her family have made.

Q. How did you come to have six children?

A. When we were first married, my husband wanted two and I wanted four—three was a compromise. After the third child, God made the decision for our fourth for us, and then God changed our hearts about family and family size. We are still open to more children, either through birth or adoption, because our desire is to be obedient to what He wants for our family. So far, it seems that having six children is what He wants for us.

Q. How and why did you decide to homeschool?

A. We never intended to homeschool. We had our oldest child enrolled in private Christian preschool by the time he was two. By the time he was four, he knew his letters and numbers and how to read. He was bored stiff in school. Then when I was very pregnant with our third child, a horrific news story came out about a fifth-grade boy needing remedial reading help. The public school's solution was for him to read out loud to a classroom of his "peers." They had him reading aloud to kindergartners. For us, this was a huge contradiction, since public schools tout that kids can learn better when they are in age-segregated learning environments with specially trained teachers. But the horrific part is that while this fifth-grade boy was reading to a classroom of kindergarteners, a gun went off in his back pocket. No one was hurt, except the boy's backside. But this was the very school and classroom that our five-year-old was about to attend.

I researched local private schools but soon realized that if we were going to send our son to private school, it would cost a third of our income. I would need to go to work to send just one child to school. We decided we would homeschool for one year. How much damage could we possibly do?

He started kindergarten using first-grade curriculum. That year, we moved twice, had a new baby, traveled a lot, and successfully homeschooled our kindergartener. We decided to do it again for first grade and then second grade. And by then, our second child was ready for kindergarten. And we were pregnant again (surprise!).

During this time, we found that not only did we really *like* homeschooling and having our kids home with us, but God had planted a firm conviction that we were to walk and talk the ways of God with our kids 24/7 and that doing anything else, for our family, would be a sin. He also changed our hearts about how to "do" family and about family size. Homeschooling became more about how God was changing us and our thinking than about knowledge we were imparting to our kids. Since then, our kids' spiritual training in all subject areas of life has become our primary concern and our primary ministry. We are very concerned about leaving a godly legacy for our children and our grandchildren.

Q. What have you had to sacrifice to finance this lifestyle?
A. A second car, a couch, and a dining room table that seats all of us. We have a loveseat, a small dining room table and a kitchen breakfast bar. At times, my husband has worked a part-time job in addition to his full-time job. He's able to work from home often, and I make appointments and run errands around his schedule, or I drive him to work so I can use the car. We spend more in gas than the average family because we travel often. But we spend less in school clothes and supplies. We spend less in activities. We buy family memberships because it's cheaper than buying individual tickets (even if we only use it once, it more than pays for itself). We don't really go to the movies. We wait for movies to come out on DVD and pop popcorn at home. We have lots of family bonding game nights and cooking frenzies.

Q. What personal sacrifices have you made for this lifestyle?

A. I can be out of the house for Bible studies/small groups or support groups only once or twice a month rather than weekly. Sometimes I want "Mommy time" or adult conversation, but I do not find this to be a *need*. I think our society has placed too much emphasis on it being a need rather than a desire.

I cannot manage homeschooling, the home, myself, and raising my kids if I am also managing an outside-the-home ministry. My primary ministry is my family. If I say yes to something else, I am saying to no my family in some area. We are willing to serve as a family in any capacity. We'll help an overstressed mom load her groceries into the car, serve in the church, or support my husband in his efforts outside the home. We'll babysit kids and incorporate them into what we are doing, or bring meals to neighbors, sick friends, or military families. Or we travel to take care of our family.

For this season, this is my primary purpose, my way of serving the Lord. It's not about secluding ourselves from the world, or being afraid of the culture, or being unwilling to leave our comfort zones. It's about obeying God for a season and intentionally raising our children the way God has led us, however imperfectly (and we do it imperfectly)!

Q. What blessings do you reap because of these choices? Are there any surprising ones?

A. It's a lifestyle of simplicity and flexibility. We can travel when we want to; we are not bound by someone else's calendar. We take cool field trips all over the country!

Our children's relationships are family focused; they don't view their friendships as more important than their sibling relationships, and they enjoy being with their parents! They seem conscious of the needs of others and are always looking for opportunities to serve our community both in and outside of church activities.

Q. How do you stay organized enough to keep everyone educated, fed, and clothed each day?

A. I don't. But some trusted organizational techniques help, and I am constantly tweaking our ways of doing things. Everyone is tasked with assignments. Being a manager of the home doesn't mean I do it all myself. It means delegating jobs and teaching tasks to the children (repeatedly, until they're mastered!). Even the littlest of our household have chores. Our little kids' dishes are kept in a drawer, for instance, so that they can put their own dishes away when they unload the dishwasher. It means arranging the dishwasher and cabinets unconventionally to achieve the purpose.

It also means keeping perspective—we can't expect the little kids to do a job the way an older child or adult will. We don't lower standards but keep proper perspective and gradually raise the standard and increase responsibility as a child ages. The long-range benefit is that my children are fully equipped to deal with the world outside our house. They see needs and are capable of responding to them, sometimes before adults do.

I also read Kim Brenneman's *Large Family Logistics* and Steven and Teri Maxwell's books *Managers of Their*

115

Homes and *Managers of Their Chores.* Lots of organizational books are helpful, but these get to the heart of a homeschooling lifestyle with larger families.

Being organized actually means being flexible to the max, it seems to me! It's an exhausting routine! But we can't manage with uncontrolled chaos. The goal is to control chaos.

Q. Do you have any support in the community?

A. We are part of a supportive and loving local church body. Our homeschool and large-family support come from several support groups and information networks in the community. We belong to a citywide information support group, a homeschool co-operative group, a large-family homeschool group, and a nationwide legal information group. We also belong to several Facebook/blogging question-and-answer type groups. Finally, we have long-distance homeschooling friends who are part of our support system.

Being in communities of believers with similar life circumstances is beneficial. But so is being around people with different life circumstances. The latter causes us to reevaluate why we do what we do, and keeps us thinking and challenging our approaches . . . which is never bad!

Q. What are the important lessons you hope to impart to your kids?

A. Their relationship with God will be their most important relationship. In spite of disappointments, losses, changes, or rejection, God never changes. What appear to be disappointing answers from God are and will be for our good. I want them to view circumstances and culture through this relationship, and make good decisions informed by the Bible, such as who they will marry. They need to test everything against the Word of God lest they be led astray by false teachers or philosophies. Finally, I'd like to understand that life is precious—all life. It should be valued and viewed the way God sees it.

MELODY'S SON ATTEMPTS TO PSYCH-OUT THE TOOTH FAIRY

My son got mad about being sent to his room, so he pulled out a tooth that *wasn't even loose* so that the Tooth Fairy would come! But the Tooth Fairy was smart. Instead of money, she left him a note explaining that she could not take the tooth because it wasn't ready yet for the Tooth Museum—it hadn't had enough time to grow. My son thought he would outmaneuver us all again by taking a dollar out of his brother's wallet. He was very proud of himself.

Needless to say, I now keep the boys' money in the bank, and my son has not tried to pull one over on the Tooth Fairy since.

CHAPTER 8

I Want to Be a Smart Mother

At some point, every mother finds herself staring at her child, perplexed. The kid has asked a question with no good answer, or pointed out something obvious about ourselves that we don't want to talk about, or pulled a stunt so incredible that we have no idea what to do. We've been outwitted by a person who can't even operate the microwave.

A quick check of the bookstore offers a faint ray of hope. The shelves bulge with helpful books on how to parent our children. Whatever ails your family, a book has probably been written for you. And yet, these books can offer only so much help. Every family faces a unique set of circumstances and no parenting book in the universe will be able to give you all the answers.

"Okay, but what do I do with this kid?!" we ask ourselves and God. If you've made it this far with me in this book, you know what my answer is going to be: read the Bible and pray for God's direction. The exciting thing is that this answer is also the solution for issues much broader than the needs of parenting. We are often pressed to make decisions for our futures, marriages, community, and churches. When we need to work through a challenge, it is comforting to know that God already has the answers and is waiting to show us the way.

Because I'm the Mom, and I Said So!

As mothers, we get to set the rules. It's one of the perks of motherhood, and this is what we longed to do when we were eight years old ourselves. Do you remember being eight? We were desperate to control the world around us. We wanted to set our own bedtime, pick our own food, and watch our own TV shows. We longed to rule the universe.

Well, my friends, we have arrived. Now we *do* rule these tiny universes, and it's not really as much fun as we had imagined. Too many dissenters are involved. I do my best to make good decisions for the kids, but often I'm lost. Is Audrey old enough to choose her own clothes? Should I make a fuss about the messy bedroom? Can Caleb stay up that late or will he be too grouchy the next day? Is this friend a good idea? What schools should we choose? How often can we ask Grandma to babysit before we're pushing our luck? Chores? Allowances? Staying home alone?

Someone has to make these decisions, and that responsibility falls to us. Decision making seemed so easy when we were eight, but as adults we often realize we don't have the first clue of what to do. Don't tell my children, but I sometimes think to myself, "I am making this up as I go. I have no idea of what to do now." Adults recognize that we need wisdom to make the right choices, and sometimes we don't have that wisdom innately. We need to talk to friends who have older children, to older mothers, and even to our own mothers. And of course, we need to read the Bible and pray for wisdom, but we'll get to that soon enough.

I Smell a Rat and His Gym Shoes

Of course we love our kids wildly. But as we love our kids with reckless abandon, let's also keep one wise eye open to the possibility that they may not be perfect. We've all seen those mothers on the news, after their son robs a bank or burns down a city, who sob and say, "But Billy couldn't have done this! He's a good boy!" And all of Billy's teachers and neighbors and guidance counselors look at her in amazement, thinking, "That kid has been a walking nightmare for twenty years and you've turned a blind eye. We're just lucky he didn't burn down *two* cities."

We're the first line of defense for our cities. If our kid is going to go off the deep end and take everyone with him (or her), let's be aware of the tendency and stop it before it gets out of control. I know I'm being overly dramatic, but you get my point. Everyone has faults that affect the people around us— our families, friends, and community. Let's work to minimize those issues in our kids while we maximize their strengths.

Take an honest look at your children—what are their weaknesses? Find them. Study them. And then find the antidote to those particular problems. I'm not advocating that we pursue perfection for them relentlessly. Criticism will harden their hearts. Instead use wisdom, mercy, and grace to understand your child's strengths and weaknesses. Then when you sense a particular problem, discuss it gently with the child and set up consequences for the behavior if it continues. Stick to the consequences, no matter what. Turn a deaf ear to whining and begging. Do not engage in power struggles. You're the parent; you have the money and keys. If you so choose, there will be no trips to McDonald's, no fruit snacks, no sleepovers, and no video games until the situation improves. Watch carefully for any signs of their willingness to deceive or manipulate. The future of your city may rest in your hands.

Let's not forget that we can never lose hope in our kids. They will mature. If they don't get the lesson the first time, they may need to learn it in different ways over time. My friend Sandy's son is now forty years old. Sandy wanted her son to be a caring, loving man who treated others well, was obedient to God, and honored Him in his life. She says, "That didn't always happen—shock!!!—but he is a wonderful man now and I'm very proud of him as a husband, father, and son."

Not Just Discipline—We Have to Train Them, Too

It may take our kids a few years to get with the program, but most of them will make it. One day they'll be the parents, police officers, teachers, preachers, judges, and nurses—perfectly sound and responsible members of society. That is, as long as we recognize that what we are doing right now will impact the future. If we skip on the discipline and teaching now, it will show in twenty years.

Whenever I don't know what to do for my kids, I look ahead to how the problem will affect them as adults. This is why I worked hard when they were very young to teach them to be independent, to solve problems for themselves, and to obey. When they are adults, they will have to be able to hold down a job, keep their own home, and be responsible for themselves. They will be accountable to a boss and will have to understand submission to authority. They will have neighbors who will need them to be considerate and tidy. They will have responsibility in their communities and churches.

All of these lessons begin right now, in our home. If I want a thirty-five-year-old who still lives in my house and expects me to do her laundry, cleaning, and cooking, I could save myself a whole lot of hassle right now and just do all this stuff for her. It's so much easier to do it myself than to train *them* to do it. But as my kids are able, I transfer responsibility to them. In Michigan a child can move to a booster car seat with a shoulder belt when he or she turns four. On my son's fourth birthday, we were out in the Buick, cheering him on as he clicked and unclicked his seatbelt until he could do it like a pro. It took thirty minutes for him to get the hang of it, but I haven't had to snap that kid into a seatbelt in years. The poor child spent the first two years of swimming lessons hollering in fear of certain drowning, but I turned a deaf ear and made him get in that pool. His swimming teacher, God bless her, did not give up on him. Now into his fourth summer of lessons he can run off the diving board and jump in the deep end without any floaties. Truly, friends, this is a miracle. But it's a miracle I would not have seen if I had given in to his temporary fears and let him choose the easy way out.

We Can't Forget Ourselves

One day our children will be out of the house and we'll be left with ourselves, our husbands, and possibly the pet tortoise that the kids begged for when they were ten, but nobody realized tortoises have a life span of ninety years, so now we're stuck with it forever. You, the husband, and the tortoise had better be preparing for the future. What are you going to do with yourself? Will you work? Will you volunteer full-time? What does God have for your future? My friend Shana says that she plans to raise her kids and then wait for grandchildren. If the grandchildren take too long, she might get a nursing degree and ask her husband to move with her overseas so she can work in an orphanage. Jenny wants to take a pottery class. Barb wants to write a moving piece of literature, like *To Kill a Mockingbird*. Deb wants to focus on her husband and building a godly family legacy.

In order for any of this to happen, we need to be learning and growing now to prepare wisely for the future. We need to build our marriages now, so that when the kids leave we still know and like that man who has shared our bed for twenty-five years. We need to plan our finances wisely now, so that we have enough to share and enjoy our lives in the future. None of this will happen if we give in to our temporary concerns and ignore what lies ahead.

No matter our situation or desires, the point is still the same. What does God want us to do with our futures? How can we start to prepare for them right now? I know it can seem like forever before we have to think about this, but time is creeping by even though we might be too busy to notice. Right now, close your eyes and imagine your future. What does it look like? Where are you? Who is with you?

What are you doing? Take a minute to pray. Ask God if this dream is what He wants for you. Most of us have several years before the kids are grown and the nest is empty. But if we start thinking and praying about our plans now, we'll have a head start on an exciting future.

Wisdom and Humility, the Inseparable Duo

As I prayed over this chapter, I asked God what He wanted me to teach. The more I prayed, the more the word *humility* came to mind. As I sat down with the Bible, the Spirit led me to several passages that clearly show a link between humility and wisdom:

- "The fear of the Lord is the beginning of wisdom; all who follow his precepts have good understanding. To him belongs eternal praise" (Psalm 111:10).

- "When pride comes, then comes disgrace, but with humility comes wisdom" (Proverbs 11:2).

- "He has showed you, O man, what is good. And what does the Lord require of you? To act justly and to love mercy and to walk humbly with your God" (Micah 6:8).

- "Who is wise and understanding among you? Let him show it by his good life, by deeds done in the humility that comes from wisdom" (James 3:13).

As mothers, we need massive dollops of wisdom. We need to acknowledge this need and admit that we are not enough. We are small, weak, and foolish in comparison to our big, powerful, and wise God. A healthy respect (fear) of Him leads us to see Him for who He is—awesome and worthy of worship. Without this humility, we can't have true wisdom. *Humility is the beginning of wisdom.* So let us make every effort to humble ourselves, realize God is smarter than we are, and seek His wisdom fervently.

But what does humble wisdom look like, and how can we apply it to motherhood? Let's take some time to study James 3:17, which says, "The wisdom that comes from heaven is first of all pure; then peace-loving, considerate, submissive, full of mercy and good fruit, impartial and sincere."

Heavenly wisdom is pure. Not contaminated. It comes directly from God without corruption from us, other people, or the culture. What does the Bible teach us in any matter? We start there. For example, the world teaches our little girls to dress like flirts and live like rock stars. God's Word tells us to dress modestly and live humble and gentle lives of servanthood. Which lifestyle will we encourage our child to choose?

Wisdom is peace-loving. Peace-loving moms don't look to prove themselves right or stir up problems for their own amusement or convenience. This may mean we let go of some issues that are not critical. I had a Sunday school teacher who used to say, "Know what hills you're willing to die on." As much as I don't understand the popularity of tattoos (I apologize to all the ink-lovers out there), I know that one day my kids may come home covered in permanent pictures and obscure poetry. I'm gritting my teeth right now, telling myself that I will choose to focus on their hearts. Are they serving God to the best of their ability? Are they kind and generous? Those are the hills I am willing to die on; the tattoo battlefield is not going to take me out.

Wisdom is considerate and impartial. Are we examining an issue from all sides? Do considerations for each child carry equal weight in our decisions? We need to ask ourselves these questions to make decisions fairly. Of course, not everyone will be happy with every decision. We'll have to make unpopular choices at times. But let's make them after we've considered each perspective.

Wisdom is submissive. I don't mean that wise parents submit to their children. As parents we have been given authority over the children. However, we can be submissive to the wisdom that God may bring to us from other sources. Authors, radio hosts, counselors, pastors, and members of our communities can teach us. If their wisdom is humble and biblically sound, we will do well to listen to their advice. It's just possible that we might not know everything. It's also possible that we may be so entrenched in a crisis that we can't see the way out. Look to other wise parents who can point a way forward.

Wisdom is full of mercy. Nothing will harden our children's hearts faster than if they see that *we* have hard, unmerciful hearts. Do we discipline them too severely? Do we expect them to fail and disappoint us? Do we subtly rub it in when they make mistakes? They will feel our underlying hostility and it will affect their spirits. Instead we need to let them see our love through their mistakes and bad choices. We must react firmly but with love and gentleness—in a way that will give them the courage to try again.

Wisdom grows good fruit. What results do we want to see from our parenting efforts? When my kids speak kindly to one another, when they share, or when they react calmly to a difficult situation, my heart just sings for joy. It's wonderful to see even the smallest good fruit that comes from parenting with God's wisdom. We've already talked about how we can't control every word, thought, or action a child might choose. We might not see the fruit of our efforts consistently. But by and large, wise parenting gives our kids the ability to make better choices. When we see those moments of maturity, we need to celebrate them. We need to thank God for the wisdom that allows the fruit to grow, and give that kid a high five, saying, "Good job, Rob! Way to not kick Stephen in the ankle after he shoved you down on the soccer field!"

Wisdom is sincere. We can preach to our kids until we're hoarse and sick of the sound of our own voices. But unless we back up our words with our actions, our kids will ignore us. Wisdom is not hypocritical. When we tell our kids to eat well, we must eat well. When we outlaw certain TV shows for them, we must also monitor our own entertainment. If we want them to serve the community, we need to be giving them an example to follow.

The next time you're faced with a big parenting decision and don't know what to do, prayerfully work through this list. You may not have a clear answer when you're done, but you will have covered biblical basics that will steer you in the right direction. Try it for decisions from curfews to clothing, pets to permission slips. God's wisdom is available to us; all we have to do is humbly seek it. James reminds us, "If any of you lacks wisdom, he should ask God, who gives generously to all without finding fault, and it will be given to him" (1:5).

It Turns Out I Have Other Problems

I learned that I am not the smartest woman in the world through my parenting experiences. That was where God first grabbed my attention and I began learning humility. Once He had my attention, He began pointing out other areas (okay, *every* area) where I don't know what I'm doing and I'm lost without Him.

As I write this, I am currently in the middle of just such a situation. I will not go into gory details, but our church has been struggling for some time and is now separating into two congregations. In addition, we've lost some families to other churches.

Eric and I were college students together in this congregation. I was baptized in the ancient baptistery we keep in the front of the sanctuary. We were married in this building on a snowy December night. Our babies spent their first Sundays in this building. (In fact, we were at church the day our son was born; he arrived four hours after the morning service.) We have invested countless hours, dollars, and effort into building relationships and following God with this church family. I miss my friends who have left so intensely that I spent a good portion of the last service in tears. I am grieving the loss like a divorce; it certainly feels like it right now.

In my calmest moments I realize that we are two different groups with two different sets of ministry goals. It's in everyone's best interest to take a break so that later we can seek reconciliation and forgiveness, because we haven't handled the separation perfectly. People have been hurt; relationships need to be mended. Many of us hope that we can regroup in some way in the future, if only for service projects and special events.

On paper this sounds so simple. In real life, it's very, very hard. We long to worship with our family but realize that's not possible at this point. And so you can find me before the almighty God, praying for wisdom, peace, direction, and healing. He has not let me down—each prayer grants me renewed peace and grace. I keep praying and He keeps granting. I have faith that this complicated situation will work out eventually.

Every Christian has faced a similar search for wisdom. Churches, jobs, moves, large purchases, legal trouble—these decisions all call for God's wisdom and direction. We don't want to rush into them with only our own understanding. Psalm 25:8–15 says,

> Good and upright is the Lord;
> therefore he instructs sinners in his ways.
> He guides the humble in what is right
> and teaches them his way.
> All the ways of the Lord are loving and faithful
> for those who keep the demands of his covenant.
> For the sake of your name, O Lord,
> forgive my iniquity, though it is great.
> Who, then, is the man that fears the Lord?
> He will instruct him in the way chosen for him.
> He will spend his days in prosperity,
> and his descendants will inherit the land.
> The Lord confides in those who fear him;
> he makes his covenant known to them.
> My eyes are ever on the Lord,
> for only he will release my feet from the snare.

Simply restated, when we realize that God is good and upright, that He teaches and guides, that He loves us faithfully and also keeps us from the snare, then we have put God in the place He deserves. Our hearts will have chosen Him as our source of wisdom, and God will be able to heap blessings on us. We'll know the right thing to do. We'll understand when we have sinned and that we're also forgiven. We will prosper spiritually and emotionally, and have everything we need. And when we are stuck in a mess, He will come to bust us out. That's what a loving God does for the children who humbly seek their Father's wisdom.

Recently I saw an example of the exact *opposite* of this on a television show. It was a classic illustration of what not to do. I was watching a show about selling homes in New York, the great hub of American real estate. A woman wanted to sell her one-room loft apartment for $500,000; her realtor told her it was worth $400,000. The woman wanted to display her idols and occult symbols because they gave the home "energy"; the realtor told her she needed to put them away to make the home comfortable to all possible buyers. The woman wanted to be present at all showings; her realtor told her she needed to be absent or at least silent while people came to see the apartment.

Her stubbornness torpedoed every possible sale. She didn't lower her price, she kept her freaky decorations, and she refused to leave when prospective buyers came. Not only did she stay, she followed realtors and buyers around her home and made herself a tremendous nuisance. She appeared so convinced of her own opinion that she never considered that she may be wrong and the realtor may be right.

You will not be surprised to know that she blamed the realtor when the loft did not sell. She seemed to have plans to sell it herself using the power of her tarot cards and the creepy idol with the knives through its head. I'm not sure how invested Satan is in real estate, but I do know he loves a prideful spirit.

Here's My Point

If you get one thing out of this book, please let it be this: humbly seek God in everything. Make seeking Him the foundation for every decision you will ever make and every attitude you will ever have because He is the source of every blessing you will receive. Recognizing God's greatness in contrast to personal inadequacy will change your life. It will open your heart and make it tender, which is the only way God can work in your life. Trust God in this. He will work a miracle in your humbled heart. I know He's done it in mine.

Study Questions

1. What parenting decisions are you facing? What information or help have you sought?
2. Think about a catastrophe caused by someone's pride. Who was affected? What were the long-term consequences? What can you learn from this example?
3. Do you parent humbly, or do you struggle with seeking input from others? How has this affected your children?
4. For further study, read James 1:2–8, 19–25 and Philippians 2:3–8.

THIS IS DIFFERENT THAN WHAT I PICTURED

I asked: Are you ever discontent with your life?

Shana answered: Sometimes I mope because I pictured myself home during the day, alone, making cookies in a beautifully clean home, or going for a walk or out for coffee with a friend. But God had other plans and I do these things with my four children in tow.

CHAPTER 9

I Want to Be a Content Mother

I have a little friend named Anna who taught herself to read when she was about four and a half years old. I was reading her a story when I realized Anna knew all the words just as well as I did. At first I thought, "Certainly this child isn't *reading*. She just memorized this book." So I found another book and pointed at words to see if she knew them. Not only could she read them, but she recognized them immediately. I finally stumped her, *a four-and-a-half-year-old*, with a word so ridiculous that *I* could barely read it. I don't remember what the word was, exactly, but I remember that I searched for a difficult one because I wanted to find the limit of this little genius headed for fame and an early doctorate in literature. When her mom returned, I asked how long she had been teaching Anna to read. "I haven't taught her!" Jenny replied. "She taught herself!" We both turned our heads and stared at the child, mystified.

Fast-forward three years, and Anna is now a reading maniac. Her parents have to follow her around the house to take books away from her so she can connect with real humans occasionally. And brush her teeth, too. Last week her mother found her staring into the bathroom closet instead of attending to her dental hygiene. "Anna! What are you doing instead of brushing your teeth?" her mother asked. "Oh, I'm just reading this box," Anna replied. The poor kid can't stop reading.

Now let's discuss my little friend Scott. The kid hates to read. He makes sure to tell me how much he hates it on a regular basis. Given the chance, I believe this second grader would drop out of school right now and become a full-time hunter. He'd move out to the woods, build himself a pine cabin, and make like Charles Ingalls from *Little House in the Big Woods.* He'd trap and hunt his own food and plant a little garden. And he'd be happy as a clam out there, with no books to upset his day.

Obviously, Anna's mom is thrilled she's a good reader. But occasionally she wishes her child could focus on other important tasks without being reminded four times to put down the book. And Scott's mom is happy that he has healthy interests and enjoys nature, but she recognizes that an education is necessary even if Scott's not interested. No child is perfect. Each has strengths and weaknesses. If we focus on a child's challenges or weaknesses, we will find ourselves sinking into a sea of discouragement and discontent. I want to encourage us to ask God for a new perspective on motherhood so we can recognize the blessings throughout our day, mature into more content mothers, and have the energy we need to continue on.

Recognizing the Blessings

How content are you with your children? Are you satisfied with who they are as individuals? Do you encourage their strengths and understand their weaknesses? How content are you with mothering in general? Is this experience turning out okay, or are you still waiting for the Motherhood Fairy to drop out of the sky and bring you satisfaction with her magic Mommy Wand? A wise mother is able to recognize God's blessings in her life, even when they come wrapped in a package she wasn't expecting.

I interviewed my good friend Becca at the end of this chapter. I hope that you'll read her words and understand the challenges that this dear woman has weathered with grace and good humor. Her oldest child was born with a genetic condition known as velo-cardio-facial-syndrome (VCFS). The condition has affected Jacob's health and development on almost every level. If I had experienced Becca's parenting challenges, I would have said, "Well, folks, this is enough. You can see I have my hands full here, so one kid it is." I would have been focusing on the challenges of parenting. But Becca and her husband see Jacob for who he really is—a precious blessing from God. Because God designed Jacob this way, his parents are at peace with it and decided to have two more children.

This is what Becca has to say about contentment:

There is no perfect life. It's so easy to be discontent with what we have (either physically or relationally), what our children have accomplished, how we look, etc. If wishes made things true, I would have never struggled with depression, anxiety over my children's health, or fear. But then I might only know the promises of God as "something I've read" instead of "something I've lived." What a loss that would be! Let me be clear: I don't believe God put these things in my life to "teach me a lesson"—they all came about because I live in a fallen world. However, "His divine power has given us everything we need for life and godliness through our knowledge of him who called us by his own glory and goodness" (2 Peter 1:3).

Becca didn't come to this beautiful, mature perspective on Jacob's situation naturally. It was through prayer and seeking God's perspective that she was able to find the strength she needed to be the mother her kids needed.

Becca can now recognize that difficulty brings a bittersweet privilege of knowing God's promises firsthand. We often feel His promises and presence most keenly in the middle of our trouble. Philippians 4:11–13 is a familiar passage on contentment:

> I have learned to be content whatever the circumstances. I know what it is to be in need, and I know what it is to have plenty. I have learned the secret of being content in any and every situation, whether well fed or hungry, whether living in plenty or in want. I can do everything through him who gives me strength.

We often apply this passage to financial matters or material desires, but let's apply it to the needs of motherhood for a minute. Would we be able to identify with these verses if Paul had written, "I have learned the secret of being content in every situation, whether my kid is at the top of his class or the bottom; thin and pretty or messy and plump; athletic and successful or awkward and socially lost. It doesn't matter what kind of kid God has given me because He will give me the strength to do this well; I want exactly the child I have."

I don't mean to negate the difficulty of parenting. It *is* hard to remain loving and supportive in the face of challenges. When the angry teacher calls, when Grandma gives the kid back with a bad report, when they are out of bed for the fifteenth time, when the bedroom is a nasty swampland that smells like rotten cheesy puffs—these are the times we throw up our hands and wish that these young'uns could get their act together. Or maybe we begin to wish that we were someplace else, like on the beach in Tahiti at dusk with a book and a giant chocolate chip cookie to keep us company.

It's natural to be frustrated occasionally, but we can't pitch a tent in fantasyland. It's important to replace the temporary stress with a long-term attitude of thankfulness for their existence. I don't think we can do this on our own; we need God's help, energy, and strength. He can move us through the difficulty and give us what we need to accomplish the job He has given us.

When Four Years Last Four Decades

I have promised myself, and I mean it, that I will never be one of those little old ladies who wander around the grocery store looking for young mothers to upset. I remember grocery shopping in the early years. I'd have Caleb strapped into the cart while Audrey was free to roam. She ran here and there, she picked up cans that were heavy enough to amputate all her toes if dropped, she bottled up traffic in the cereal aisle, and she begged for plastic toys. Caleb just wailed in misery. Invariably some tiny old lady would come up to us and say, "Oh, I remember those days. Treasure this time; they grow so fast." And I would smile through gritted teeth and promise to treasure every last minute of this beautiful time, wondering if she had forgotten the reality of young children or if her kids were far easier to raise.

So my new ministry is to empathize with young mothers in the grocery store. The worse their children are behaving, the more apt I am to walk right up them to let them know that my kids used to do the very same thing. Sometimes I even throw in the story about the time that Caleb screamed through Meijer (an enormous store) for more than an hour. The whole place was relieved to see us go, I'm sure.

While I'm talking to these women my children are now standing next to me, listening to this story and giggling. They no longer scream in the cart. They no longer run in circles and crash into other shoppers. They do still beg for plastic toys and still drop gigantic cans sometimes, but the whole experience is much more pleasant because they have grown out of that early phase.

These years really are fleeting, I promise you. But while I was in the midst of them, I could see no end. I didn't realize how quickly they would grow into responsible kids who could understand why they had to behave in a grocery store. I was so overwhelmed; I was lost in the moment. It never occurred to me to ask God for His perspective on the situation. Yes, I know *now* that those challenges were temporary because kids grow up in the blink of an eye. But I could have learned the lesson a whole lot faster if I would have asked God for His perspective then.

So, my friend, if you are reading this chapter and thinking, "I would be more content if my life wasn't so hard every minute of every day," I don't mean to aggravate you like the well-meaning older ladies. Just consider me a beacon of hope on the other side of the river, signaling that it's all going to be okay pretty soon. And maybe you can learn from my lessons, and let God teach you now instead of later.

I May Have Been Placed in the Wrong Neighborhood

As far as I can tell, my small town consists of six gardeners, seventy-five book lovers, one hundred exercise enthusiasts, and one thousand eight hundred nineteen NASCAR fans. You can guess which club gets my membership card. Some days I wonder why God put us here. We'd love to live in a town with a cavernous library and museums. Recently I walked through town and boldly asked God for direction on where we should live. Does He really want us here, living in town with close neighbors? Really close neighbors who enjoy replacing the engine to their beat-up old Civic *all night long*? Really? Haven't I put in my time in this starter house, and isn't it about time I get to move to a house with real bedrooms and a place to put muddy boots? I don't think I'm being unreasonable, but I'm also sure I haven't learned my lesson in being content, so God is continuing to teach (and reteach) me.

I have learned many foundational lessons about contentment from motherhood, and I've been able to mature in many ways from those lessons. But I have to relearn contentment every single day. Every day I wage a battle against discontent—with my kids' current phases, with my house, with my furniture, with my Buick, with my clothes. It never ends for me.

This is not to say that I'm not making progress. I love certain things about this little town: we have wonderful staff at the library and grocery store, and our schools are fabulous. We even have an annual nighttime Christmas parade with fire trucks decorated in thousands of tiny Christmas lights. I have several great walking routes around my safe neighborhood and many great neighbors who *don't* rip out engines in the middle of the night. There are many things to be thankful for.

That day when I walked and prayed about moving, God answered me clearly. He told me that we are here because we need to be a part of this community. My only obedient response is to be satisfied with that answer, and then to repeatedly choose satisfaction with His plan every time I feel the discontentment monster creep in.

As followers of Christ, we must always choose to be satisfied with God's presence and plan for our lives. David says in Psalm 63:1–5,

> O God, you are my God, earnestly I seek you; my soul thirsts for you, my body longs for you, in a dry and weary land where there is no water. I have seen you in the sanctuary and beheld your power and your glory. Because your love is better than life, my lips will glorify you. I will praise you as long as I live, and in your name I will lift up my hands. My soul will be satisfied as with the richest of foods; with singing lips my mouth will praise you.

Notice that David sought God's presence and glory. He ached for a simple glimpse of his glorious God. His soul burned with thirst that could be quenched only with living water (John 4:9–14). Do we seek God as fervently as David sought Him? I can't speak for you, but I know that often I crave a new couch or a new pair of shoes with more emotion than I long to sit in God's presence.

I wouldn't be surprised at all if this is exactly why God keeps us in unsatisfactory places. When we can't have what we want, the ache grows stronger in our hearts. We will only find contentment and satisfy that longing when we take our eyes off the earthly problem and decide to worship the eternal God instead. I could buy a new couch once a year and it still wouldn't satisfy that craving deep in my soul. David put his focus on God's glory, and it took away the emptiness that he could never fill on his own.

Relentless cravings for possessions, comfort, status, security, or pleasures keep us searching and restless—always peeking into closed doors and wondering "what if," always hoping our cravings will be filled by magic. "More, more, something different!" our spirits cry. Well, my spirit, here is what will satisfy your longing: seeking God's presence, His direction, and His plan. Seeking Him will move us away from our self-centered grasping and into a place where He can lead us to peace and satisfaction. Sometimes He changes the circumstances that have us so upset. More often, He changes our hearts and we realize that we were the problem all along. Proverbs 19:23 says, "The fear of the Lord leads to life: then one rests content, untouched by trouble." We will still have trouble, but it won't affect us the same way when we focus on pleasing God.

The Energy to Carry On

Our focus won't change naturally. When we find ourselves mired in discontent and disappointment, we need to purposefully choose a new perspective with God's help. He will not disappoint us! No matter how real the problem may be, how difficult, or how permanent, He can help us find a blessing in every situation.

It's often little blessings that give us the energy to continue. Some days my kids put up a fight about *everything*. They don't want to get out of bed, brush their hair, eat breakfast, or brush their teeth. All this strain, and it's only 7:32 a.m. But then I remind myself about my friend Stacy, who would be thrilled if her son could get out of bed by himself. If he could brush his own teeth, she'd cry for joy. The simple fact that my kids have the ability to fight me on this stuff is a huge blessing, even though it doesn't feel like it.

I'm working hard to identify the blessings. Let me list a few of them for you: I am thankful my son will finally eat chicken and/or beans, because this has cut our family dinner tension in half. I am thankful my daughter learned to brush her own hair. I love the way Caleb still holds my hand every once in a while, when he forgets how big he is. I am thankful they have outgrown all those mind-numbing baby shows. I love how they smell when they are freshly out of the shower and snuggled in clean pajamas. I am thankful for the noise and the chaos, because the alternative would be clean, lonely silence.

Now it's your turn. Make your own list, and tack it the refrigerator door if you need to remind yourself hourly. May God give you His perspective to find the daily blessings.

Study Questions

1. What makes you discontent as a parent? Do these issues legitimately require change, or do you need to make peace with them?

2. If something about your child bothers you, consider what will happen to him or her if it doesn't change. Will your child grow to be a happy and functional adult, or will this inhibit him or her if it isn't corrected?

3. What lessons have you learned about contentment from parenting that translate to the rest of your life? What have you learned that has helped you grow closer to God?

4. Outside of parenting, what discontentment issues do you face? What do you need to do about them?

5. Do each of your kids have a challenge that is gently stretching them right now?

6. For further study, read Psalm 34:8–10; Ecclesiastes 4:8; Isaiah 55:1–3.

AN INTERVIEW WITH
MY FRIEND BECCA

Becca and I have known each other since elementary school. She and I weathered junior high and high school together, kept in touch through college, and now live twenty minutes apart. I asked for her input because her path through motherhood has been profoundly affected by her son's genetic condition. I hope that her story will encourage you as much as it encouraged me.

Q. Please explain Jacob's genetic condition.

A. Our firstborn child has a genetic abnormality called VCFS (velo-cardio-facial syndrome), which is caused by deletion of part of the twenty-second chromosome. Soon after he was born the doctors discovered some abnormalities in his heart that worried us. When he was a preschooler we decided to have his genes tested at the recommendation of his cardiologist and discovered that he has VCFS. We are so blessed that in the subsequent months and years after diagnosis Jacob has escaped many possible symptoms of VCFS.

Q. How does Jacob's condition affect you as his mother?

A. It's heartbreaking to feel powerless to help my child. I waver in hope that he will have basic joys in his future that other parents take for granted for their children. However, I am relearning how to expect a good future for my son. God says that His plans for us are good!

Q. How did you decide to have more children? What health concerns have your children faced?

A. My husband, Matt, and I had to decide whether or not we wanted to undergo genetic testing before we had another child. We knew that any child we conceived we would love and treasure, but we also had to think about the odds of having another child with special needs. In our case the odds were low, so we decided to forgo genetic testing and trust for healthy babies. We were so blessed to welcome two other children to the world. Our third child had a cardiologist visit while she was still in utero, and she received a clean bill of health. We have now "graduated" from cardiology with all three children, which is an enormous blessing.

Q. Where have you found support for Jacob and yourself?

A. My husband is the best daddy our son could ever wish for. The number of families who stay together with special needs children is low. I'm so glad that my husband is such an amazing father. I couldn't imagine parenting without him. I'm also incredibly blessed that our son has a great aide to help him through his school experience.

Q. What has been encouraging to you in the last seven years of motherhood?

A. I love looking through our "family journals" and watching movie clips that I've made of my son to see the growth and progress he's made. He has grown phenomenally, and I think it's important to celebrate positive change. I'm trying to remind myself that the same accomplishment in two different children is often achieved through completely different amounts of effort. So I celebrate my children's wins. It's worth it to pause and reflect on how many mountaintops we've already scaled.

Q. What is your most frequent prayer for your family?

A. I have had more cause to pray for health and healing than I would have wished. However, I have also seen God answer those prayers in amazing ways. Jacob was born with a hole in his heart, an artery that "looped" around his esophagus and trachea, and palate issues that make eating and drinking difficult. As he grew we realized that his speech was delayed. We spent many hours during his preschool years with speech pathologists, ophthalmologists, and cardiologists. All of this was before the VCFS diagnosis. We clung to the promise of God that "the stammering tongue will be fluent and clear" (Isaiah 32:4). Our son is now in first grade; he is speaking clearly; the hole in his heart closed without need for intervention; the "loop" never interfered with his eating, drinking, and breathing; his body is growing stronger; and he is a great reader. The journey is not over yet, but we have seen amazing progress in his development and we give all the glory to God. We live according to Psalm 56:3: "When I am afraid, I will trust in you."

Q. Is there anything else you'd like another mother to know?

A. As one mama whose precious child has been labeled to another, I would say this: if you wonder whether you will ever find someone who sees your child as you do—someone who loves your child beyond measure and who sees all the amazing, beautiful, precious things about your child that you do—remember your God. In my grief I wondered, "God, do you love this precious one like I do?" God was okay with my questions and tears. But He loves me enough not to keep me in suspense. He reminds me that He loves my child so much more than I can imagine.

I remind my children of this regularly. I sometimes ask them at night, "How much does Mommy love you?" They hold out their arms and say, "This much!" And then I ask, "And who loves you even more than Mommy?" "God!" they shout. It's as much a reminder to me as it is to them.

God loves you; God loves your child; God is a good God; God's plans are good.

SERIOUS ABOUT FINANCIAL RESPONSIBILITY

I asked: Can you tell me about your family's finances?

Sara answered: If we can do something ourselves, we do it and don't have it hired out. This works well because my husband, Dayton, is extremely handy. He built our house and barn, which saved us a lot of money. He then built an outdoor wood-burning furnace so we can heat our house inexpensively. Dayton also changes the oil in our vehicles and rotates tires. I cut the boys' hair, and sometimes the girls' as well. I love hand-me-downs, garage sales, and clearance racks. We enjoy going out to eat as a family but try not to do it too often since that can really add up. We try to pack lunches instead.

CHAPTER 10

I Want to Be
a Financially
Stable Mother

My family likes to go to the neighborhood park, and because I work at the school, kids there often recognize me and launch into long and complicated monologues. Many times I have no idea of who these children are, specifically speaking. One day my husband and I were greeted by a boy of about eight years old, at the park all by himself. He was riding a bike in circles and having a fine old time. He rode up to us and proceeded to explain in detail what was wrong with the bike.

"Look at these wheels. They're rusting. And I don't like the handlebars. And the paint is chipped here, and here, and here. I got this bike out of my aunt's basement, and I want a new one soon. I don't like this one at all." I pointed out that the bike looked fine if a person didn't inspect it and reminded him that even new bikes eventually get old. I also pointed out that it could have been painted purple or hot pink, so really it wasn't so bad.

He did not agree. He had worked himself into such a state about the bike that nothing about it pleased him anymore. I sighed and gave up, hoping that my own kids would never be so ungrateful for their things. And then the Holy Spirit said to my heart, loudly and clearly, "This is how you feel about your house, missy." And I got that nasty feeling in the pit of my stomach because I suddenly realized how blind and dumb I had been. This is *exactly* what I do to my house. I have friends over and I walk them through it, showing them every detail that bothers me. I'm sure that God is no more pleased with my whining than I was with the boy and his bike.

Our financial choices are often based on our contentment. In this chapter we'll discuss the need to be financially stable mothers, but we're just extending the discussion in the previous chapter on contentment. I firmly believe that we cannot be financially stable mothers if we are not first content mothers. When our hearts are at rest with God's plan and provision, then we will be able to make good financial decisions.

With that said, money affects every mother. It doesn't matter if we're a single mother living in subsidized housing with four children, a stay-at-home mother who homeschools, or a mother of one child enrolled in a boarding school in France. We've all been given resources and we have to manage them to the best of our ability. I believe God is watching us closely to see if our attitudes are right, if our decisions are wise, and if we are trusting in His ability to provide for our needs. The amount of money He has given us is not the issue—we are the issue.

Picture Money as a Shovel

Shovels are tools. So are forks, forklifts, and food processors. So, for that matter, are houses, credit cards, clothing, incomes, and cars. They are all designed to do a specific job. But at some point we decided that certain tools can somehow define us, proving or disproving our worth to ourselves or others. Have you ever gone into your grandpa's shed and yelled, "Oh, Grandpa, I can't believe you have this fabulous shovel! This is the newest model—where did you find it?! I'm going to buy one *right now*."

No. You haven't done that because it's ridiculous. If you need a shovel you go to the nearest store that sells shovels. You find the one that will do the job for the least amount of money. Or maybe you find the one that was made in America, whatever. You take the shovel home, you dig up the ground with it, it gets dirty, and then you hang it in the shed. You don't show it to your girlfriends when they come to visit, you don't slyly fit into the conversation that you have a brand new shovel, and you certainly don't secretly wish for your neighbor's shovel. Because, again, that would be ridiculous.

I don't know why we've decided as a society that some tools carry more status or stigma. Yet we accept these values as our own when we buy things to impress people (whether or not we can afford them), or flaunt what we feel is special and hide what embarrasses us. We inadvertently teach our children that possessions have more value than God intended.

The early church had the right attitude. Acts 4:32–35 reads,

> All the believers were one in heart and mind. No one claimed that any of his possessions was his own, but they shared everything they had. With great power the apostles continued to testify to the resurrection of the Lord Jesus, and much grace was upon them all. There were no needy persons among them. For from time to time those who owned lands or houses sold them, brought the money from the sales and put it at the apostles' feet, and it was distributed to anyone as he had need.

Believers used their money and possessions to make sure everyone had what they needed. They focused on evangelizing, sharing, and spreading God's love. They were so excited about the gospel that they didn't waste time quibbling or hoarding.

Also notice that the early Christians moved past good intentions and blessed others through good management. We'll talk more about this, so remember it. Individuals put land up for sale, completed the transaction, brought the money, and gave it to the disciples. Then the leaders decided where it was needed and made sure it was distributed. The needy were needy no longer because everyone had the right attitude and followed through in obedience. Good and faithful management is a blessing to everyone involved.

What Do I Choose?

Identifying our financial attitudes and motives will lead us to the right decisions about money. For example, do I really need a new car because the old one is too small or unreliable, or am I trying to impress the other moms at preschool? Am I buying this doll for my daughter because she loves it, or because I want her to have the same brand that all the other girls have? Does my son need these shoes because the coach said he must have them, or am I just adding an unnecessary pair to his collection? In every situation the financial choice is neutral. Cars, dolls, and shoes are just items we buy and use. It's not wrong to buy them, nor is the purchase inherently good. However, what motivates us to make that decision or purchase can be good or bad.

My husband and I wrestle with our motivations frequently. We try not to spoil our children. We don't want them to grow up assuming that everything they want will be handed to them, but it can be hard to find a balance between spoiling them and unfairly refusing purchases. It's possible to go too far in either direction. We want to find middle ground where our children have what they need and some of the things they want, so they learn healthy attitudes about money and possessions.

We have friends who live in an upper middle-class neighborhood, and their kids are the only ones on the block who don't have motorized scooters. They have perfectly good old-style scooters, but they want the same ones as the neighbors. Their mom can understand why. The other kids zip around on the streets while her kids puff behind them, powering their scooters with their little legs. She wonders, "Should I buy my kids fancy scooters so they will fit in, or is it good for them to learn to make do with old scooters?" I can empathize with her dilemma.

These types of dilemmas require that we have financial priorities or goals, which will help us make decisions. Though we should all strive to have pure motives when making decisions, motives don't always point to the right choice for our families. That's why parents have to determine their priorities. Let's examine the working mother issue as an example. Of course, single mothers rarely have a choice. If they don't work, no one eats. Simple enough. But the issue gets complicated for married parents. Dual incomes might be a permanent need or a temporary solution. Sometimes the cost of living in an area is so high that it takes two incomes to meet basic expenses. Other times a second income is needed in homes affected by disability, lack of education, or a bad economy. We also have families who just plain want to have two working parents. Perhaps the mother wants to work, the family is saving money for a specific goal, or the wife makes far more money than her husband and he still wants to work. In cases where working is optional, couples have to determine their priorities and goals to make the decision about whether a parent works or stays home.

Those mothers who choose to stay home often sacrifice all luxuries and many comforts as a result. Several of my friends commented on how priorities influenced this choice for them. Do they miss the big new houses and the shiny minivans with automatic rear doors and entertainment systems? Yes, sometimes they do. But Shana commented that "going to one income seemed impossible, but it has been the best thing we've ever done." Melissa said, "We made the choice for me to stay home when my first daughter, Jordyn, was born. That time was a huge blessing. If I could do it again, I would quit work and be home while the girls were growing up."

I don't want to start a debate on the merits of working in or out of the home. My point is that families have to evaluate what is important to them financially, and then work hard to fit the priorities within their financial reality. My working friends rarely have homes that smell like freshly baked bread, and sometimes they squeeze in their quality time with the kids between school and hockey practice on Tuesday nights. My stay-at-home friends sometimes wish they could go to the store and buy the expensive bread and not have to worry about the seven dollars it costs. But when families are committed to having the right attitudes about their money and the plan God has for them, each choice can work out well.

In God We Trust

Printed on United States cash are the words "In God We Trust." I find this ironic because Americans are awful at trusting God when it comes to money. Actually, we don't want to trust God for anything, so we have a pocket full of cash (if you're over sixty) or a wallet full of cards (if you're young and hip). We're never without a single thing we want or need, as long as we have a credit card to ease us through the week.

Do we trust God with our finances? Let's think through this carefully.

- How much do you have in your savings account? Are you hoarding the amount in case God fails you? Or are you simply saving responsibly with an eye to the future?

- Let's pretend that your car and house burn tomorrow and you had to move to a cheap apartment, drive a cheap rental car, and buy clothes at the thrift store until your insurance check arrives. Would you be embarrassed? Would your friends even notice the change? Are you trusting in your possessions to give you significance, or are you trusting in God?

- How many of your purchases are specifically aimed at making your life more comfortable? This covers everything from entertainment to whether or not your kids have to share a bedroom. Are there times when you can't share generously because you have made too many commitments to your comfort?

- Has your family experienced the blessing of tithing firsthand? Countless families can testify that when they give to God, He gives back in amazing ways. Do you trust Him enough to give?

I know, I know. We're modern. We're with the times. We can't be sitting around on the farm and watching the beans grow. I understand. I admit that I have a snazzy new cell phone and we're saving for a new leather chair. Again, it's not wrong to buy things. But it is biblically problematic to distrust God by taking our finances into our own hands and assuming that God doesn't need to be involved.

Hebrews 13:5–6 says, "Keep your lives free from the love of money and be content with what you have, because God has said, 'Never will I leave you; never will I forsake you.' So we say with confidence, 'The Lord is my helper; I will not be afraid. What can man do to me?'" That's a good question. What can man do to us? He can mock us, make us feel inferior, and have more bedrooms than we do. But if we are daughters of the almighty God, we are in a very secure position. We need to remember that. We choose to follow God's financial directions because we trust that He will not leave or forget us. Our needs will be met.

I think many of us know this in theory. The Bible says that we can trust God, so we believe it. But do we really trust Him? What does that look like? A mother who trusts God prays before making financial decisions. If she thinks that a purchase would not please God, then she doesn't buy it, no matter how much she or her children may want it. She trusts that God sees the bigger picture and has her family's best interest in mind.

A mother who trusts God obeys biblical financial guidelines, not the world's. She tithes, pays her taxes and bills, takes care of her children's needs, saves for the future, and shares with others. If there is money left over, then she can take an occasional trip to the mall.

Finally, a trusting mother is always honest with God, herself, and others as she makes financial decisions. If we can't afford something, then we shouldn't buy it. If we owe other people money, then we pay them before we buy extras. If taxes are due, we pay the taxes in full. Dishonesty brings us stress and frustration but trust in God brings us financial freedom that will bless our children.

Under New Management

Let's go back to the subject of good management. We saw in Acts 4 how the early church's financial management was a blessing to the believers. As mothers, we have the same opportunity with our families. We are the managers, which means that we allocate our resources for the best use in the home. A good manager can still live an amazing life on limited resources.

We live near a mobile home park that I like to walk through occasionally because a few houses lift my spirits. The owners have taken their modest places and planted flowers, pulled weeds, and accessorized with birdbaths and wind chimes. The homes are welcoming and charming. Good management does that for a home, whether it's a mobile home in a blue-collar neighborhood or a majestic home on the lake. Good management ensures that not only are the family's needs of shelter, food, and clothing met to the utmost of the resources God has given, but that the home is also welcoming and inviting to guests. That's what God asks of us, that we use our resources wisely and share generously.

Good *intentions* are not enough. Until we follow through on what we know we should do, we aren't being good managers and our families will suffer for it. Consider this, if you were paid to manage an office and you handled it just like you manage your home, would you be fired or promoted? Many of us have worked under bad managers. No matter how nice that boss may be, if he or she cannot keep the supplies stocked, the schedule organized, or paychecks written on time, then no one wants to work for that person. It's just too frustrating. How are our management efforts affecting our families?

Good management also keeps an eye on the future. We aren't promised that tomorrow will be as bountiful as today. Are we planning for that? The book of Genesis (chapters 39–41) talks about Joseph, a man who had a God-given talent for good management. Joseph started small, in Potiphar's house. Because of Joseph's faithful management, Potiphar didn't have to worry about anything in his household—Joe was on the job. The servants were organized and fed, the pantry was full, the cattle were happy, and the buildings were in good repair. God blessed Joseph and he worked diligently. Everyone was blessed because of him.

A few years later Joseph was given a new responsibility. He correctly interpreted Pharaoh's dream about Egypt suffering a severe famine, and Pharaoh put him in charge of the kingdom's famine preparations. When the famine came, Egypt was ready. Joseph had directed the farmers in each community to store excess grain in their cities.

Did it mean that the Egyptians had to make some sacrifices during the bountiful years? I think it did. Genesis 41:49 says, "Joseph stored up huge quantities of grain, like the sand of the sea; it was so much that he stopped keeping records because it was beyond measure." I'm sure some Egyptian somewhere complained long and loud about how he could be selling this grain for a profit instead of adding it to the giant heap in the community grain bin. But I bet that same man was mighty happy to have food instead of profit when the earth stopped producing. The sacrifices required in wise planning are rarely pleasant, but they're necessary.

We need to note that Joseph's rise to power did not happen immediately. God tested Joseph's heart in challenging situations. First, his brothers sold him into slavery because they hated him. Joseph did not let bitterness ruin his life. He chose to work hard, and God blessed him. Then he was unjustly accused by Potiphar's horrid wife and thrown into prison for years. He was even forgotten in that jail by those who said they'd put in a good word for him! How many of us could survive betrayal, slavery, unjust accusations, and years in jail and come out better for it? Joseph did it, and I think that's why God blessed him and others through his life. When we are faithful through bitter pain and still bless others, then we are excellent managers.

I don't know about you, but I'm feeling like an underachiever right about now. Still, God has called us to be good managers where we are, to bless others with the resources we have been given. Most mothers are in charge of purchases for the family. We buy the shoes, the groceries, and the clothes. To do that we need to know how much we have to work with. Do you have a good idea of your family's income and expenses each month? Good managers know that information and work to keep the expenses as low as common sense allows. We work to meet everyone's needs while setting enough aside to share with others in need and to save. We do not spend every penny in bountiful times because we never know when the economy is going to tank again or the job will be lost. But we also do not live in financial fear, because we know that we have chosen to the best of our ability and we trust God to provide the rest.

Apparently Marriage Means Sharing

Most mothers don't make financial decisions alone. Married women have husbands as financial partners. Divorced and single mothers often split costs with the children's father through legal or informal child support. No matter the situation, God has called us to make financial decisions *with* integrity and *without* selfishness. This is where the rubber meets the road, girls. We can talk about spiritual things all day long and sing praises to God at the top of our lungs, but this is where we put our faith into action. How are we handling the financial decisions with our partners? Do our attitudes and choices reflect God's love for our brothers?

If we go to Ephesians 5:22–24 we learn the following: "Wives, submit to your husbands as to the Lord. For the husband is the head of the wife as Christ is the head of the church, his body, of which he is the Savior. Now as the church submits to Christ, so also wives should submit to their husbands in everything." *Everything* does include the money, honey. These three verses in Ephesians can be difficult for our modern minds to accept, so if your hackles are up right now take a few minutes to read Ephesians 5:22–6:9. You'll be comforted to know that every Christ follower is called to submission: wives, husbands, children, and slaves (or employees). God didn't single out the wives.

Ephesians 5:22–24 covers a marriage relationship, but we also need to look at 1 Corinthians 11:11, which says, "In the Lord, however, woman is not independent of man, nor is man independent of woman." Simply put, our choices affect one another whether or not we are married. What we do as women affects everyone around us. The surrounding verses in the eleventh chapter of 1 Corinthians have challenging teachings (on women's hair length, head coverings, and proper etiquette at communion) that have been interpreted in different ways throughout the generations and cultures. However, I see a theme throughout the chapter: Be considerate of your brothers and sisters in Christ. Make every effort to respect them and behave in a way that does not offend them.

These are hard teachings! It is not in our human nature to submit, nor to accept that our choices affect others. Money issues bring this out in us. Some of us may be married to men who make, ah, *interesting* financial decisions. You are reading this section with a growing sense of panic. "You don't understand! If I let my husband make the financial decisions, we'll be *living* in that stupid bass boat by fall!" That concern may be justified, but God has called you to submit to your husband, and further, to trust in God himself. We do not put our faith in our husbands. In reality, this is barely about our husbands! This is about submitting to God with our whole beings and learning to seek His best for our lives.

I know a couple of wives who have put their trust in God and let their husband make the financial choices, even when all evidence indicated that it was going to be a challenge. I am happy to report that usually it takes a man only one really hard lesson before he changes his ways. Some of the men were allowed to sink under the weight of their bad decisions, but God has not let anyone in the family drown. Everyone has come up, lived through it, and learned a powerful lesson. I'm sure the wives would have been more comfortable temporarily if they had controlled the situation. Sometimes, however, we put ourselves in places we do not belong to protect our husbands from a lesson that God needs them to learn. Take a minute to pray about this idea and how it might be affecting your marriage. Are there areas, financial or otherwise, where you are interjecting yourself between God and your husband?

This is not to say that we get to, or have to, sit back and let men carry the financial burden alone. God gave us brains and opinions that we need to use in *helpful* ways. As financial managers, we also carry responsibility. Most of us have a better grip on the actual cost of raising our kids. For example, ask your kids' dad right now: How much do gym shoes cost? How much do school pictures cost? How much does a school lunch cost? Probably you will get a blank stare from the poor man. Most men have no idea. My husband doesn't know those things, but he does know, to the penny, how much we earned, saved, and spent last week. It behooves us to work together! Our children live a life of financial peace and blessing because Eric and I work really, really hard to agree on these matters. Do I have everything I want? No.

Does Eric have everything he wants? No. And neither do the children! That's how it works in our house—no one ever gets everything he or she wants.

The world may view this situation as misery. And to be honest, for a few minutes each day, one of us pities the fact that we do not have a new couch, classic car, or roller coaster in the backyard. However, Christ calls us to lay down our lives for others. We're called to set aside our selfish wants and to trust Him for our deepest needs and desires. Because God's Word promises God's blessing when we do things His way, I implore you to give this a try.

Right this minute, think of one financial choice that you could make in a better, more God-honoring way. Maybe you could stop plotting and begging for a new minivan and be content with the car you have (I preach to myself). Maybe you could downsize your house so you have more money to give generously. Maybe you could ask for your husband's opinion on a financial matter and quietly live with his decision. Don't forget to pray for the wisdom to make the right choice and for His grace to give you the strength to abide by His direction.

I don't know how this will work out for you, but I do know you will not regret it. Trusting God is rarely comfortable, but it is never regrettable. God will provide, He will teach you, and He will be with you through the process. I pray you'll give Him the chance to prove this to you!

Study Questions

1. Here's a pop quiz:
   a. What is your family's monthly income?

   b. What are your average monthly expenses?

   c. Are you able to give generously to your church and others in need?

   d. Do you have a system for saving money, and do you stick to it?

2. What was the last financial decision your husband (or children's father) made? Did you agree or disagree? How did it work out?

4. How do you decide whether to buy your children things they don't *need*?

5. For further study, read 1 Chronicles 29:14; Matthew 6:25–34; Mark 10:17–31.

SIMPLE ORGANIZATIONAL TRICKS FOR FAMILIES

- Keep down the clutter. If you don't need it, get rid of it right away. Especially all those cheap trinkety plastic toys that seem to attach themselves to our kids. Your kids won't miss them and you don't need to feel guilty for not keeping them. —Jenny

- As soon as you find out about something, write it on your calendar. I have a large calendar so I can fit lots of information each day. I also have a notebook that I keep in plain sight to keep track of what we need for school, the weekly menu, and my to-do list. —Sara

- Make the kids feel like organizing and cleaning is their idea. —Grandma Freda

- Get ready for Sunday morning on Saturday evening by ironing clothes, making kids take baths, and putting shoes, Bibles, etc., all in one place so they're ready to go. —Melissa

- Teach your kids to do simple chores. When my son, Steve, was in middle school, I showed him how to do laundry. That was very helpful to me since I worked full-time. He also vacuumed and dusted on occasion. Because he did those things, we were able to spend more time together and have more fun together. The bonus was that when he lived on own, he already knew how to do all those things. He makes a good husband, too! —Sandy

- Start a seasonal to-do list instead of a daily list. It gives me no joy to write, "food, laundry, dishes, cleaning" on a list and check items off each day; it's just a written reminder that my career as a full-time mom is rather repetitive. However, it gives me great joy to write a list of big or fun projects that I want to do in a season, like "get Emma potty trained, remodel office at church, plant some flowers." I find that when I plan for a season it gives me more grace on when things get done and more ability to match my list to the energy and time I have. —Sara

• Give everyone their own laundry basket to put their dirty clothes in. The clothes get folded and put back in the baskets, and then go right back to the kids' rooms. —Shana

• Plan ahead for meals. We work together as a family to make a menu for two weeks. Then we make a grocery list. This cuts back costs and we can make sure that we have everything that we need. —Melody

• Give everyone their own color. I wrote each child's activities on the calendar in their color and their laundry basket was that color. They each had a clip on the fridge in their color to keep soccer schedules and other papers. —Barb

• Keep simple photo albums for each child. I've kept up with putting their photos in them. I didn't put in comments, but the photos were all in one place in chronological order so they could have them as adults. —Barb

CHAPTER 11

I Want to Be an Organized Mother

My childhood was deeply affected by the presence of three elderly ladies: my maternal grandmother, Josephine, and her two sisters, Annie and Helen. Someday I will write a book about them, but this will have to do for now. Born into the Polish-Catholic community of Detroit in the early 1900s, they religiously attended mass and confession. They were prone to bickering, and occasionally nagged in English, sometimes in Polish. Their arguments blew up from out of nowhere and died down just as quickly. They often got loud, and I learned a lot of exciting words when they fought. They tempered their fighting with absolute devotion to one another and a deep sense of kindness. Love was regularly dispensed in doses of doughnuts and cabbage. But not together. No one ever made me eat cabbage for breakfast.

Lest you have no experience with Detroit's Polish-Catholic community, let me note that cleanliness and organization are highly valued. My mother still shudders at memories of cleaning days from her youth. These women would work themselves into a frenzy for hours to clean every crevice, tile, floor, and shelf. Nothing escaped their notice. Boxes were labeled and neatly stacked in the basement. Knickknacks were kept to a bare minimum and stored in a fancy cabinet. If you couldn't organize it, you didn't keep it. End of story.

My great-aunt Helen had the strongest personality of the sisters. She never did anything halfway, whether it was expressing her opinion or generously sharing her material goods. Some of her best stories were the ones she told me about her relationship with her husband, Uncle Joe. (Uncle Joe had a glass eye, which never closed while he slept. I just thought you should know that to get a good picture.) As Aunt Helen grew older, she got a bit overzealous in the organizing area. We lovingly called her "The Claw." If she saw something out of place, she took it and put it where it belonged. Occasionally she forgot where she put it. So, for example, if you put your purse on the kitchen counter, good luck finding it in thirty minutes when you need to leave. Good luck finding your keys, your scarf, or your coat. Adios, flip-flops.

As I age, I find myself developing this habit of hers. Just two days ago I had to e-mail my daughter's teacher to apologize for throwing away her unfinished homework. I throw away paystubs and need them later, old shoes just because they are in my way, and boxes from the basement without looking in them first. Every few months I eye my neatly boxed wedding dress and fight the urge to get rid of it. Does anyone need a fourteen-year-old wedding dress? I'll give it to you, for free!

I realize this habit makes me sound weird, but the four of us are living in a house of nine-hundred square feet. We don't have the room to store stuff that we don't need. I'm trying to teach my kids this principle, and I think they're catching on. Audrey is now starting to evaluate whether she needs to keep every toy, and Caleb is good about not buying too many things. They are starting to understand that being organized makes life easier for everyone, and you can't be organized if you have too much stuff.

Wading through the Clutter

Modern life tends to get complicated. We have all this stuff, and it comes with more stuff. For example, if you have a car you need keys to operate it. Now think about the rest of your key ring: You need keys to get into your job, house, and sister-in-law's house when she locks herself out. You also need a beeper thing to unlock the trunk from twenty feet away and a canister of pepper spray. And you probably also need a decorative key chain of some sort, to remind you of your children's names or of your vacation to Aruba last year. And this is just our key rings! When we multiply this by all the areas of our lives, and then multiply it again by the number of people in our families, we find ourselves stacked to the neck with piles of accumulations. Baseball equipment, ballet outfits, homework folders, Girl Scout packets, and ten years of accumulated Christmas toys—am I alone, here?

Contrast this with early Native Americans. They had a tepee, which didn't even have a locking door. And they had a canoe, which definitely didn't have an ignition. I don't know if they needed mementos of vacations or not. And I certainly don't know where they kept them if they had no keys to lose three times a day. Their lives were hard, but simple. Modern life might demand a wide range of possessions, but this is in stark contrast to life in the thousands of years before us. And even today, people in many areas of the world live with few possessions.

In reality, we don't need much to survive. Jesus said, "Therefore I tell you, do not worry about your life, what you will eat or drink; or about your body, what you will wear. Is not life more important than food, and the body more important than clothes?" (Matthew 6:25). Jesus referred specifically to food and clothing; He didn't even mention towels, dishes, lawn mowers, baseball cleats, doll houses, hot tubs, or computers. We own a lot of things that don't sustain our lives.

Instead of making our lives easier, our possessions may entangle us and make them more difficult. How much time do we lose each day looking for something we or the kids need? How many boxes in our basements have not been touched since we moved in ten years ago? How many toys do our children own that they haven't played with recently? If you look around your house and feel a vague sense of drowning panic set in, this is the chapter for you. My Polish heritage is here to help you clear out this stuff. If my genetics aren't enough to convince you, let me reassure you that I'm basing these ideas on Jesus' words in Luke 12:33: "Sell your possessions and give to the poor. Provide purses for yourselves that will not wear out, a treasure in heaven that will not be exhausted, where no thief comes near and no moth destroys."

Organizing in Action

Pick whatever room most bothers you. It will be the one where the kids dump the most stuff and you are always embarrassed when a visitor sees it. Find a few hours and pile everything together that isn't attached to a wall. Get under the furniture, into the deep corners, and dig out the closets and drawers. Now that you have a giant pile of dusty stuff in the middle of the room, go get a giant garbage can and keep it close. Start sorting, and *show no mercy*. Throw out anything that is broken. Throw it right away. If you haven't had it fixed yet, you've obviously been living without it and you don't need it. It's like ripping off a Band-Aid, ladies. Do it fast and it doesn't hurt so much. Out it goes!

You should also start a pile of items that are used regularly—every day or so. Get rid of any multiples that you don't need, however. No one needs twelve spatulas or ten pairs of flip-flops! The extras go into the giveaway pile.

We also need a pile of things that aren't used every day, but are needed at specific times. For example, Christmas decorations, off-season clothing, or sunscreen. Don't throw away what you will need later just because you don't need it now (yes, I preach to myself again).

Finally, make a pile for items with emotional attachment, like your first grader's journals from school. Nobody *needs* those things, but even my Polish people keep that stuff. We'll just get a nice box for it and neatly label it for the basement. And then as soon as your child has a home of her own, the box gets dumped in her garage. Neatly dumped, of course.

Now that we have all of our items sorted, we put everything where it belongs. We take the garbage out right away; we do not keep it around for a few days so we can think about what's in there. We put the things we use every day in the now empty drawers or closets where we can find them the fastest. (Grandma Josie would recommend washing down those surfaces before you put stuff back, but use your own judgment.) We buy huge plastic tubs for the seasonal items and store them out of the way. And, of course, we put the emotional mementos in their own boxes and places for later.

Now you will have lost five or six valuable hours of your life, but you will have one clean room and you will feel better. Repeat this process through your whole house in the next couple of months. Then, and this is the important part, keep doing it each year. If you keep up with this process, you will never find yourself overwhelmed by an entire house full of loot. You'll have a tidy house. You'll be able to find everything you need quickly. And your children will be able to find what they need, while they learn an important lesson in how to manage their own household one day.

Wait, Wait, We Forgot a Pile

We need to talk about the most important pile, the giveaway pile. You should be able to generate a large amount of stuff that someone else could use. Think generously if you're having trouble making a decision about what to keep. For example, perhaps we find ten sweaters in our dresser. Even if you live in the tundra like I do, no one needs ten sweaters.

Because our culture is so bent on accumulating as much as possible, we rarely slow down to think about how much we need to live a modestly comfortable life. I'm not advising that we go back to the days when people had only two sets of clothing, but I am advising that we prayerfully consider how much we have at our disposal. If we go back to Luke 12:33, Jesus told us to sell our things and give to the poor. How are we doing with that?

This doesn't go for just sweaters and small appliances that we cheerfully give to the Salvation Army. Some of us may need to think bigger. Do we have anything large taking up our time, money, and space unnecessarily? What about RVs, hot tubs, extra cars, or boats? If your family enjoys these things and uses them frequently, then they are probably worth keeping. But what if the item is barely used? Barely enjoyed when it is used? Selling that item might be a double blessing. You could get rid of it and free up time and space. It's liberating to release yourself from material weights hanging around your neck. But if you take that money and give it to someone in need, then you've doubled the blessing by passing it along to others. It's something to think about, at least. Certainly something to pray about.

I Hear a Ghostly Polka in the Distance

Quiet—do you hear that? Do you hear my Polish relatives dancing in glee from the other side? Now that you've decided to clear out your clutter, they're having a party and dancing with their accordions to the polka. You've made them so happy! Your family will be more comfortable and able to stay organized. You've taught your children how to separate important possessions from the not-so-important. And you've taught them to be generous.

Well, so what? Plenty of godly mothers never clean a closet in their lives. They die with piles of things for their kids to get rid of, and their children are happy to do it because their mother loved them fervently.

Let's look at two Scripture passages to take this subject a little deeper. In Luke 9:1–4 Jesus sent out the twelve disciples to begin their ministries:

> When Jesus had called the Twelve together, he gave them power and authority to drive out all demons and to cure diseases, and he sent them out to preach the kingdom of God and to heal the sick. He told them: "Take nothing for the journey—no staff, no bag, no bread, no money, no extra tunic. Whatever house you enter, stay there until you leave that town."

In Luke 12:35–38 Jesus says,

> "Be dressed ready for service and keep your lamps burning, like men waiting for their master to return from a wedding banquet, so that when he comes and knocks they can immediately open the door for him. It will be good for those servants whose master finds them watching when he comes. I tell you the truth, he will dress himself to serve, will have them recline at the table and will come and wait on them. It will be good for those servants whose master finds them ready, even if he comes in the second or third watch of the night."

Eric and I have two sets of friends who are missionaries. Both couples heard God's call to the mission field and began to prepare. They sold most of their things and put a few special pieces into storage. They rented their homes and sold their cars. They pared down belongings until they had only daily necessities. Then, while they still waited on God, one family rented a tiny apartment and the other moved in with Grandma and Grandpa. When the time came to move, they were ready. Nothing held them back because they had taken these two passages to heart.

Christians with obedient hearts do not get ensnared by their possessions. They prepare and stay organized so that no matter what God asks them to do, nothing material will stand in their way. If God asks us to make a meal for a new mother, then we get into the kitchen and do it because our kitchen is stocked, clean, and ready to go. If a missionary needs a place to stay for a few nights, we have clean sheets, a reasonably tidy room, and a kid who can sleep on the couch. If we need to move to Alaska to join a ministry, then we're ready to rent the house and sell the couch because we are listening, watching, and ready.

We are to live lives of joyful expectation. What is God going to do through us today, this week, this lifetime? He has a great plan! But we need to focus on seeking it and being ready for it when it comes. Think of what would have happened to the disciples if they had ignored Jesus' directions. What if Thomas had said, "I'm going to need that extra tunic. It gets cold at night and some of these families don't have extra blankets. And no reasonable man travels without his staff, because how else can I fight off wild dogs or rude Samaritans? And, of course, I'm still going to take my own money. Not taking it would be ridiculous." He would have missed the whole point, which is that God provides for His servants; they don't provide for themselves. And Thomas's extra belongings would have slowed him down and given him something extra to worry about. Jesus wanted His people focused on the goal—driving out demons, healing the sick, and preaching about the kingdom of God. He did not want Thomas digging through his bag, looking for his extra shirt and some coins so he could buy an afternoon snack.

We never know when God will call us to action. Luke 12:38 says that it is good for a servant to be ready, even if the master doesn't come until the middle of the night. God's timing is rarely convenient from our perspective. Our friends were willing to move to the mission field long before they actually got to go. But they sat tight and waited until the timing was right. While they waited they did not start re-buying items to make life comfortable again. They did not get distracted and lulled into permanent inaction.

I Think He's Talking to You!

Some of you are sitting on your couch, and you've squeezed your eyes shut and plugged your ears with your fingers. "If I can't see God, then He can't see me." Ha! I've tried that, ladies. It does not work. God is talking to you, and He's saying the same thing today as He was yesterday and the week before. He's calling you to action, and you know you're not prepared. Even worse, you know that getting ready will be uncomfortable.

I almost didn't write this chapter. I know that being organized is hardly a biblical mandate for a mother. God does not care if our canned vegetables are organized, and you will not find any Scripture to convince me otherwise. But the more I prayed about this chapter, the more I needed to put it in.

God is calling a few of you to a specific task, and you need to prepare. So, my dears, get ready. Because He loves you, He will get you to move. It will be far more comfortable if you move yourself, rather than if He has to pick you up and do it for you. We've all picked up a stubborn two-year-old and strapped her into her car seat while she screams. Let's not be the two-year-old. Let's be the obedient child who is watching and ready to move, not entangled in her own plans and possessions. Obedience brings blessing and God's favor.

Study Questions

1. What did your family teach you about organizing and cleaning? How does your life reflect that?
2. What items in your home could be shared with others? Toys your kids have outgrown? Extra clothing? Furniture stored in rarely used rooms? Which local ministries or organizations would put them to the best use?
3. If God called you to Africa, could you be ready in three months? What would you have to do to make it happen?
4. What is God calling you to do? Are you already moving in obedience, or sitting on the couch humming to yourself, trying to hide from God?
5. For further study, read Matthew 25:1–13 and Luke 12:15–21.

PLACES WE DREAD TAKING OUR CHILDREN

- To the mall with teens. Too much pressure to buy expensive things! And to get professional photos done for younger children. It was always stressful trying to keep the kids clean. —Barb

- To the doctor. I'm always waiting for the kids to say something like "We're going out for fries and a Coke!" when the doctor asks if we limit soda and juice. —Shana

- To that restaurant that shall remain nameless with the games and flashing lights and loud music. —Sara

- To IEPs, or Individual Education Planning meetings for special need students. If you know a mom with a special needs child, offer to go along to watch the child. These meetings are enough of a challenge without having to care for a child during them. —Sara

- To a gift shop with lots of glass and other breakable items. —Karen [Author's note: This was my mother's answer, and I'm pretty sure I was the problem. But maybe my brother or sister had something to do with it. I guess I can't take all the blame.]

- To the dentist. When we took our son to get a cavity filled he started bawling and screaming and would not let anyone touch him. —Melody

- To the grocery store! I feel like we take up too much space if we're all together. —Sara (Jenny added, "The kids dance in the aisles and pretend to be ballerinas or fairies. While this is cute, it doesn't speed up the process any.")

- To potluck suppers that are outside, or inside someone's small house with carpet. Corralling the younger kids and getting them to eat in a timely fashion is nearly impossible. —Deb

- I have always loved going anywhere with my girls, even when they were young. —Melissa

- I dread going out to eat because Lauren won't stay at the table. She likes to "work the room" and say hi to everyone. I'm not sure where she gets that! —Sandy [Author's note: This is most likely a genetically inherited condition. *That's* where she gets it.]

- To public bathrooms—they touch everything. YUCK. —Jenny

CHAPTER 12

I Want to Be
a Fearless Mother

I used to watch the news regularly, but I don't do it much anymore. Instead I watch copious amounts of the Weather Channel. Blizzards I can handle, but rape, murder, kidnapping, genocide, and economic crashes keep me up at night, wondering if I should build a shelter in the backyard to protect my children from roving bands of hungry, evil thugs. And as if the news isn't bad enough, I just read a book about the five-year Nazi occupation of Guernsey Island, where the islanders really did have to worry about protecting their children during terrible circumstances. The Nazis cut off all trade and communication with the mainland and seized anything of worth. Food became scarce. Firewood was depleted. The schools were run by Nazis. Any transgression, no matter how small, could result in a sentence to a concentration camp. That kept me anxious for *days*.

One of the marks of maturity is accepting that evil exists in the world, and then calmly going about our business anyway. I was twenty-four years old on September 11, 2001, when planes were turned into weapons. I watched the news and saw the buildings fall and the people run screaming in the New York streets. Then I watched the airline industry nearly shut down, and the economy roll in panic. My husband works in the aerospace industry, and he soon found himself without a job and without prospects for a new one because so many people were in the same position.

I'd like to say that I was mature enough to calmly go about my business anyway, but I was only twenty-four years old! And I had known twenty-four years of peace, harmony, and economic blessing. Fear and panic were new to me. I didn't handle them especially well. At the time I worked as a secretary for a unit of wonderful social workers. The blessed little helpers, they wandered around the office all day counseling people whether we wanted it or not.

I don't know what I would have done if I had been a mother at the time. My distress might have been multiplied to a strength that paralyzed me. Could I have left the house that first week? Would I have ventured to the grocery store? I'm not sure. It's one thing to fear for ourselves, but situations seem much more dire when we consider our children.

Even in times of peace we worry. We fear for our children's physical safety in cars and on the street. We worry about them socially in school, or at the playground. We fret about their health and their futures, including what governmental, economic, and environmental problems they will inherit.

In part, this concern is our duty as mothers. Understanding reality motivates us to be the best parents we can be. We know what car crashes can do to a body, so we snap our kids into their giant car seats with five-point harnesses, even when it's a hassle. We know what poor social skills will do to a person, so we work hard to teach our children good manners and how to make friends. We educate them for years to give them the best possible shot at a good income. There is no shame in preparing our children for the real world and protecting them from undue danger. That's our job and we do it well. But no matter how real the dangers of life may be, we need to move past our fears to seek God's protection, provision, and plan for our children and ourselves.

What about the Boogey Man?

Daily we cope with danger by preparing as much as possible, and then letting fear go. For example, we strap the baby into the car seat, and then we drive to the store. We know that a car seat isn't a guarantee that our child will be safe. It's simply the best protection available that allows us to maintain a normal life. We cut up his hot dog to the recommended size, knowing that he could choke no matter what we do, but the kid has to eat something. We watch our toddlers vigilantly in the bathtub, but we understand that turning our backs for five seconds could be enough time for them to slip and get a lung full of bathwater. We evaluate the risks and make the best choice, hoping that we are doing the right thing.

The wisest among us realize that we're still inadequate, even with all of our planning and safety gear. We know the boogey man is still out there, waiting to thwart us. So we run to the only One who can thwart the boogey man. "Protect this tiny person, God!" we cry. "They don't sell car seats made of titanium!"

A BLESSING TO SING OVER YOUR CHILDREN

(Courtesy of Sara, who sings this and personalizes it for each child by adding any characteristics promised by God.)

> God's plans for Hannah are good,
> God's plans for Hannah are good,
> He desires for you,
> Joy and peace
> Love and strength for always
>
> May His plans come to pass
> As He guides all your ways
> May you listen to His voice
> To the end of your days.
>
> Oh, the Lord's plans for Hannah are good.

Lifting up our children in prayer is a time-honored tradition. Mordecai, David, Zechariah, and Elizabeth all prayed for their children, among others. First, let's look at Esther and her father-like cousin, Mordecai. Esther 2:7 tells us that Esther was an orphan, so her older cousin adopted her as a daughter. The two of them lived in King Xerxes' kingdom, Jews among foreign people. Esther was chosen to be Xerxes' wife; he did not know she was Jewish. Haman, an evil and powerful man, got Xerxes to sign a law to have all of the Jews killed. Mordecai knew that Queen Esther was the only person able to get their people official protection. He said to her, "Do not think that because you are in the king's house you alone of all the Jews will escape. For if you remain silent at this time, relief and deliverance for the Jews will arise from another place, but you and your father's family will perish. And who knows but that you have come to your royal position for such a time as this?" (4:13–14).

In modern-day terms, let's say that your daughter was the president's new wife, and that Christians faced legal massacre. Would your first thought be, "Hey, she's in a great position to get us all out of this!" Nope, I don't think it would. I think most people would wobble between two panicky plans: 1) I can go live with her and at least our two lives might be spared, and 2) If I die at least she'll be spared if she stays quiet. For all we know Mordecai did consider similar plans. But whatever his initial thoughts were, he realized that eventually Esther would be found out and killed along with everyone else, and that God was powerful enough to do something very big through Esther.

Esther replied to her father-cousin, "'Go, gather together all the Jews who are in Susa, and fast for me. Do not eat or drink for three days, night or day. I and my maids will fast as you do. When this is done, I will go to the king, even though it is against the law. And if I perish, I perish.' So Mordecai went away and carried out all of Esther's instructions" (4:16–17). Fasting is an intense kind of prayer, the kind where you bring your entire body into an awareness of the almighty God. When you fast for three days you fight hunger and, more than physical discomfort, the desire to give up. Mordecai was willing to do this for Esther's sake, and for their people's sake, because he understood the deliverance that God alone could bring.

Notice that Mordecai did not try to save Esther; he let God be God. Neither did he try to downplay the problem to comfort her. In fact, he pointed out that it was not only her life but the lives of her family and friends that depended on her courage. And finally, he let her do her part and act responsibly. He did not try to interfere with the plans and manipulate the situation for her.

How does our parenting stack up against this model? When hard times come for our children, are we stepping back and letting them work it out with God? Our tendency as mothers is to step in and protect and comfort. While at times this is perfectly appropriate, other times this instinct hinders their growth or manipulates a situation for our own comfort, or to relieve our own anxiety. Prayerfully consider where your choices fall in this area. Are your actions in line with God's plan for your child's life? Esther's discomfort was necessary to save her people. Your child's discomfort may help him or her grow. I encourage you to pray for each child, and let God work where and how He chooses.

Lord, This Project Is Too Big Without Your Help

Now I want to visit another portion of the Old Testament, 1 Chronicles 29, which details David's preparations to build the temple. He had saved long and hard and had gathered the craftsmen who would make it a beautiful place to honor God. He knew that he would not build the temple himself, as God had made that clear (1 Chronicles 22:7–8). In 1 Chronicles 29:10–20 David thanked God for the provisions and ability to build the temple. He worshiped and exalted God, and humbled himself and the people. At the end of the prayer he slipped in this little request: "Give my son Solomon the wholehearted devotion to keep your commands, requirements and decrees and to do everything to build the palatial structure for which I have provided" (v. 19).

I am no expert in ancient monarchies, but I understand that succession was a bloody and complicated affair. It seems that every king had someone breathing down his neck, waiting to slay him and take over the kingdom. If I was King David, my first prayer for Solomon would have been for his safety and for the protection of his throne. But David instead prayed that his son would follow God's commands *wholeheartedly*. He knew wholehearted devotion would be the secret to Solomon's success or failure in life.

This is an important lesson to remember as our children move forward into God's callings for their lives. Right now one of us is parenting the future president of the United States of America. One of us is parenting a budding scientist who will discover the cure for cancer. One of us has a kid who will redevelop the world's educational system, and one of us is parenting the next Billy Graham. What should we be praying for? Let's start by praying that our child will follow God's commands wholeheartedly. There's nothing God can't do with a person who humbly submits to His Word.

Again with the Child and the Plan!

Now we move to the New Testament, to the book of Luke. Zechariah was a priest, an old man married to an old woman named Elizabeth. Together they had served the Lord faithfully for years, but they had no children because

Elizabeth was barren. One day while Zechariah was on duty burning incense in the temple an angel appeared to him and said,

> Do not be afraid, Zechariah; your prayer has been heard. Your wife Elizabeth will bear you a son, and you are to give him the name John. He will be a joy and delight to you, and many will rejoice because of his birth, for he will be great in the sight of the Lord. He is never to take wine or other fermented drink, and he will be filled with the Holy Spirit even from birth. Many of the people of Israel will he bring back to the Lord their God. And he will go on before the Lord, in the spirit and power of Elijah, to turn the hearts of the fathers to their children and the disobedient to the wisdom of the righteous—to make ready a people prepared for the Lord. (Luke 1:13–17)

I'm going to go out on a limb and guess that this is not exactly what Zechariah and Elizabeth had prayed for. They probably hadn't prayed for a child for many, many years. What older woman still asks for a baby? Many of us know people who just send the kids off to college when—surprise!—a new pregnancy pops into the picture. Suddenly plans are rearranged. Instead of golf weekends and romantic getaways, it's back to delivery rooms and middle-of-the-night feedings. Retirement plans are exchanged for playdates and sleepovers. It requires a completely new mind-set.

Elizabeth and Zechariah were probably just as stunned as modern-day parents in this situation. I like how the angel Gabriel said, "Your prayer has been heard." Then he calmly informed the priest of how God was going to answer this prayer that Zechariah and Elizabeth probably laid to rest long before.

I'm assuming that Zechariah and Elizabeth had hoped for children at the typical time, like everyone else. Not only did John arrive decades later than requested, God's life plan for him was very different from what his parents would have planned. In those days, sons were usually trained in their father's profession, so John would have been raised to be a priest. The angel let Elizabeth and Zechariah know that John would live a completely different kind of life, instead preparing the Israelites for the coming Messiah. Gabriel's news did not jibe with either parents' intentions or the culture's expectations.

So what about us? How do we respond when we pray for our children and God answers our prayers in ways we had never anticipated? Because we are human, we have a limited vision of what's going on. We don't know what the future will bring. We don't know exactly what weaknesses our children will develop or what strengths they will need. We certainly don't know what God's plans are for them or for the world. This shouldn't stop us from praying for them, of course. But when God answers, we need to be open to whatever He plans.

It can be scary when our plans are rerouted. What if an angel appeared in your house and gave you specific directions for your kid's life? Would you panic, or would you follow Zechariah and Elizabeth's example and trust God? It may have been frightening for them to buck the trends of their culture. They may have feared judgment from family and friends. And they may have worried over John's future or God's unusual expectations of him. But they chose to be flexible and allow God to do His work, and in doing this they were able to take part in God's work themselves. God may be asking the same from us. Do we trust Him with our children's future, or do we hang on to our fear?

An Example Straight from Jesus' Lips

I love a good summary. When a teacher can cut through all of her words and just give me one example to follow, I'm a happy woman. Lucky for us, we have just such a model in John 17. Jesus was well aware that He was about to be arrested and crucified, which is what makes His next action so significant. He started to pray for everyone. He prayed for His disciples, for us who would come after them, and for himself. John 17:6–15 records part of the prayer:

> "I have revealed you to those whom you gave me out of the world. They were yours; you gave them to me and they have obeyed your word. Now they know that everything you have given me comes from you. For I gave them the words you gave me and they accepted them. They knew with certainty that I came from you, and they believed that you sent me. I pray for them. I am not praying for the world, but for those you have given me, for they are yours. All I have is yours, and all you have is mine. And glory has come to me through them. I will remain in the world no longer, but they are still in the world, and I am coming to you. Holy Father, protect them by the power of your name—the name you gave me—so that they may be one as we are one. While I was with them, I protected them and kept them safe by that name you gave me. None has been lost except the one doomed to destruction so that Scripture would be fulfilled. . . . My prayer is not that you take them out of the world but that you protect them from the evil one."

Jesus noted repeatedly that the disciples really belonged to God. The same is true for our children. We may be raising them, but God breathed life into them, He gives us the financial resources to keep them housed and fed, and He gives us the wisdom to raise them. We have no ownership of these small folks! They belong to God and He just includes us in the process. What a relief! Have you ever met your husband at the door and said, "Do you want to know what *your* son did today?" When times get tough we can also meet our heavenly Father in prayer and say, "Can you please help me with *your* son today? I've got nothing, here. I'm done. Please take over, because I need a break."

This does not mean that we are without responsibility, of course. In this prayer Jesus stated that He had taught the disciples God's Word. He had protected them and given them the Holy Spirit to lead them. But rest assured that if we do our part, God is willing and able to handle His children.

In verse 15, Jesus does not pray that God will remove His disciples from the world or difficult situations, but that God will provide for them when they do experience trouble. I've mentioned it before, but it is so important that it bears repeating—it is not our job to protect our children from every difficulty in life. Life is hard. We let our kids experience its difficulty in small doses while they are children so that they can grow stronger as they grow taller. If Jesus himself asked for protection for His friends, not ease, then this is crucial. We must apply the lesson to our own kids and act accordingly.

Remember That We Are Still Children, Too

As mothers, we will find ourselves in difficult situations, but we need to remember that God is watching and waiting to provide what we need. We are still God's children, no matter how tall or old we get. As a result, God asks us to grow and mature and trust Him, no matter how scared we may be to follow Him, no matter how uncomfortable we may get.

Some of us are doing our best to be brave and follow God wherever He leads us. Those of us who have tried will agree—it's not easy. I have been in a few places lately where, despite my best efforts, I have completely failed or the results have been dismal. Is anything more frustrating or confusing than working hard for God and yet feeling like a failure? It can be scary to venture out there for Him.

I don't know why God doesn't solve our problems for us or bless our every effort to bear fruit. I have a sneaking suspicion that it will all work out in view of eternity, but that doesn't stop the frustration now. When you face challenges and disappointments, Psalm 20:1–9 may bring you some comfort:

> May the Lord answer you when you are in distress; may the name of the God of Jacob protect you. May he send you help from the sanctuary and grant you support from Zion. May he remember all your sacrifices and accept your burnt offerings. May he give you the desire of your heart and make all your plans succeed. We will shout for joy when you are victorious and will lift up our banners in the name of our God. May the Lord grant all your requests. Now I know that the Lord saves his anointed; he answers him from his holy heaven with the saving power of his right hand. Some trust in chariots and some in horses, but we trust in the name of the Lord our God. They are brought to their knees and fall, but we rise up and stand firm. O Lord, save the king! Answer us when we call!

God doesn't want us to fight this battle alone! I don't know your particular circumstances or what you may be fighting.

You could be dealing with health problems, a failing marriage, or children who are not responding to your parenting. Perhaps you're facing serious financial trouble or your extended family is in turmoil. God is ready to send support and help. He wants to make sure that His soldiers have what they need to be victorious.

Note that Psalm 20 does not give us an out. David did not say, "Hey, when you are in distress just go ahead and bail. God will understand." No, verse 6 says, "Now I know that the Lord saves his anointed; he answers him from his holy heaven with the saving power of his right hand."

We have God on our side! We need to live fearless lives, knowing that our heavenly Father is with us. He may have sent us into this battle directly, or perhaps He allowed it to envelope us, or maybe we got here by our own stubbornness and bad choices. It doesn't matter why we're here, it only matters that we fight well and let Him equip us for victory. We aren't trusting in horses or chariots. We trust in the name of the Lord our God. He will not fail us.

Never Forget to Pray

Life scars us all one way or another; no one exits without experiencing difficulty. So whether the need is for our kids or for ourselves, we need to pray every day. We pray for protection and direction. We pray that God works through us, even when it's unnerving and we'd all rather be home, safe and sound. Everyone, big and small, has a place in this world. God gives us tasks and we need to develop the courage to do our part. If we rely on our own strength and courage, we're bound to fail. If we rely on our kids' strength and courage, we're bound to die of heart attacks from the anxiety.

Let's take these tasks right back to the one who assigned them to us and ask for the help we need to do them! God will bless our children. He will bless our efforts. He will protect us, provide for us, and bring glory to himself. What an honor that He lets us participate in His process!

Study Questions

1. What are your children afraid of? Are those fears justified?

2. What are you afraid of? How does it affect your life?

3. Put yourself in Elizabeth's shoes. How would you feel if you found yourself pregnant in your elderly years? What if God gave you specific directions that differed from your expectations?

4. Are you open to whatever future God may have for your children? What ways are you helping them to prepare for independence? Are you preparing to let them go when it's time?

5. For further study, read Isaiah 35:3–4; John 14:25–27; Philippians 4:6–7.

AN INTERVIEW WITH MY FRIEND BARB AND HER KIDS

Barb and I have been friends for more than ten years. She and I worked together at our church and her son, Rob, was also on staff with us as the youth minister. I had a chance to see how Barb interacted with her adult children—Rob, Betsy, Stephen, and Kelly—and how her whole family loved one another. Simply put, I want my family to one day have what Barb's family has. They love each other fiercely, cover all quirkiness with a hefty sense of humor, and support one another daily. Each of the children has a personal walk with Christ and is active in church. Here is what Barb and her children have to say . . .

Jessie: Your family is so close and supportive, even though everyone is grown and has moved away. What did you do to develop that when they were young?

Barb: I tried to emphasize that family relationships are with us forever (even though we have been blessed with great friends who are like family), so always stay close to siblings. My mom drilled that into me, too. It's generational!

Betsy: Mom didn't let us play with our friends on certain occasions for no other reason than she wanted us to play with each other instead. I have strong memories of listening to Mom and Dad read to us and playing board games as a family. That has reaped a bunch of kids who really love and enjoy each other, and their parents. Also, Mom and Dad have always had big hearts for service. They brought us to a mission and nursing homes to visit with the residents and Dad took us to a children's home where we'd play soccer with the kids.

Stephen: From Mom and Dad, we learned the importance of building a family through spending time together. Mom did not have a job so that she could be at home with us. Dad worked hard, but only within an eight-hour day, never putting work before his family. Dad coached our soccer teams, Mom taught us, and they both read to us and came to our sports games in high school. We took road trips and ate dinner together. It was never about possessions and money; it was about relationships and family.

Jessie: Your married children each have a wonderful spouse. How did you manage *that*?

Barb: God is good! We are thankful. My kids just kept believing that there was someone out there who could be a wonderful mate, someone easy to be with and who would take good care of them, and that they could have the same goals and priorities—and there was!

Jessie: Did you raise your children like your mother raised you?

Barb: My mom was Catholic, and she raised my brothers and me in the church. It was a big effort for her to bring us all to church week after week without my dad, who did not go to church. My mom's faithfulness in this left a strong impression on me. She made it a regular, consistent part of my life, and I have tried to do the same for my kids. But she did not really talk about God in our everyday lives, and growing up I did not understand what it meant to know Jesus personally.

My mom never complained that we did not have much money, and sometimes when I was in school she would go back to work so we could get a color TV or because we needed a new car. She helped my dad and seemed very content. She had a kind of sophistication about her because she was from Australia and had grown up in a large city. She was always friends with people from other countries, and she was well-read and encouraged me as a young girl to read. She also was very into keeping close to your family and encouraged us to do this. I think part of this is because she left her family behind in Australia and all she had was us and my dad's family.

One thing I did differently than my mother was apologize to my children when I was wrong. I don't remember my mother ever doing that. When I was a young mother I heard a radio program on how important it is to apologize when you make mistakes. It keeps your children's hearts tender toward you. I remember being offended by my parents' lack of ability to admit when they were wrong. I think it was an authoritarian parenting attitude of their day. They thought that if you admitted you were wrong it would show weakness. In fact, the opposite is true.

My mom took excellent care of her family, she was very loving toward all of us, and she was a lot of fun. She had a great sense of humor and I hope I have inherited some of it.

Jessie: Looking back, what lessons did you emphasize?

Barb: "A wise man learns from his mistakes; a wiser man learns from the mistakes of others." I must have said that a million times! And, "Treat others the way you want to be treated"—the Golden Rule.

If they were being punished I would say, "Don't lie to me; your punishment will be much worse if you lie to me." I found it really easy to lie when I was younger and it can get you into so much trouble in life. Someone who lies just cannot be trusted and loses all credibility when caught in a lie. It's much better to own up to anything bad you have done than to lie and cover it up. The cover-up is always worse than the initial sin.

My husband, Bob, modeled dependability. He has never been a day out of work since we were married, even though we've had some close shaves and some crazy moves. He has always held a job and been responsible to take care of us all. And he also modeled *fun* for the kids!

Rob: Mom taught us to take the best things from your parents and to try to avoid inheriting their faults! She also taught us to not let other people get our goat, which I'm still working on. I also remember her telling us that it was okay to confide in other people if there was something that we couldn't talk to our parents about.

Kelly: Mom taught us to be nice to one another because our home is a safe haven for us all, and she emphasized that following Christ is the most important thing in life.

Jessie: What do you wish you would have known or done differently as a young mom?

Barb: I wish I would not have been so uptight. I wish I would have enjoyed it all more because it is gone in the blink of an eye; it really is. I am forever grateful to God for letting someone like me—so undeserving—have and raise these four kids and see them marry such nice people. Now I have grandchildren on the way! Amazing!

Despite My Shortcomings . . .

It was almost ten years ago when I started to wonder if I really knew what I was doing. The larger my pregnant belly swelled, the more concerned I became. Now I know, and you know too, that I knew *nothing*. I had a vision of what it meant to be a mother, but no real idea of what it was going to be like. I have bumbled my way through this experience, praying that God will see my love for my children and do for them what I cannot do. His provision has given me direction and wisdom where I have fallen short as a mother.

This should not be a surprise to anyone because God has been doing this exact thing for thousands of years. Do you know the story of Naomi? Naomi was a mother whom God blessed beyond measure. We find her in the book of Ruth. Frankly, I'm not sure why this book isn't called *Naomi*. It's really her book, and Ruth is kind of a young, beautiful secondary character. Poor Naomi's life was a study in crisis. Her husband and sons died, leaving her without financial support. Because she was living far away from family in a land where she had no resources, she decided to move home to Judah, and Ruth went with her. When they arrived in Judah they still faced difficult times. Ruth went to a field of a relative farmer, Boaz, and gleaned the wheat left behind after the harvest. Most of us know that Boaz married Ruth, which provided a secure and comfortable home for both women.

In the last scene of the story Naomi was caring for Ruth's newborn son, Obed. The women gathered around and blessed Naomi, saying, "Praise be to the Lord, who this day has not left you without a kinsman-redeemer. May he become famous throughout Israel! He will renew your life and sustain you in your old age. For your daughter-in-law, who loves you and who is better to you than seven sons, has given him birth" (Ruth 4:14–15).

The ending is so beautiful that it's easy to read this story and gloss over the intense emotions that Naomi must have felt in the middle of her trouble. Only a few verses touch on her pain. In Ruth 1:13 she said to her daughters-in-law, "It is more bitter for me than for you, because the Lord's hand has gone out against me!" And then when she made it back to Judah and the women were excited to see her she said, "Don't call me Naomi . . . call me Mara, because the Almighty has made my life very bitter. I went away full, but the Lord has brought me back empty. Why call me Naomi? The Lord has afflicted me; the Almighty has brought misfortune upon me" (1:20–21). It's possible that she had nursed her husband and sons while they died. The grief and inadequacy must have enveloped her. Likely she stared at her emptying purse and wondered how much longer she could go without income. The panic and anger at God must have been fierce. Maybe she sat down with Orpah and Ruth and tried to plan a new course, only to come up confused and hopeless.

Can we relate as mothers? I think we can. We have felt grief, loss, inadequacy, panic, and confusion. Because we have Ruth and Naomi's full story we know that God had not left them, and in fact was orchestrating their lives to be part of the most blessed genealogy ever known. Baby Obed grew up to be King David's grandfather! God had not deserted Naomi. Not only did the Almighty provide for this mother's needs at that moment, but He also gave her the extreme honor of writing her into a book of the Bible where His grace toward her has been encouraging God's people for thousands of years.

God's Grace toward All His Children

As we conclude our time together, I'd like to leave you with another thought from Barb. She says, "Somewhere along the way I started to pray that God's grace would fill in the gaps of my (or our) bad parenting. I know God has done that because we had some pretty bad parenting exhibited along the way!"

I love to hear Barb say that! From the outside, I see her family's success and I assume that it was some magic formula that ensured amazing kids. Did Barb and Bob work hard to raise this family? Yes, they did. They poured time and attention into their parenting. They sacrificed material comforts and career goals. They set a God-honoring foundation, homeschooled, coached soccer, and saved for college. They gave it their all.

But over it all, God poured His grace on their family. Neither Barb nor Bob are superhuman. They have quirks and limits to their abilities and patience, just like the rest of us.

I know that in my own family, as my siblings and I get older, my parents occasionally look back over the early years and wonder out loud if they did well enough. They keenly remember the difficulties and the bad days, the times when the right thing wasn't clear. But they also worked hard and loved us fiercely; God's grace was on our family.

We have a running joke in our family, one we've been repeating every few years since 1985 or so. As we sit together at the Thanksgiving table, my brother sneaks giant blobs of meat into my sister's soda. She finds it as she tries to take a drink, quietly sucks in her shriek, and then smacks him under the table, while I sit and shake in silent laughter. During all of this, my father (ignoring the fact that his grown children are acting like fools) is praying the blessing over the food my mom worked so hard to prepare.

God's grace, poured out over family. Families aren't perfect, neat, or tidy, but covered in grace nonetheless. May His grace fill the gaps in your parenting, may His encouragement move you forward, and may His love bring you closer to the foot of the cross.

Acknowledgments

To Barb, Becca, Deb, Grandma Freda, Jenny, Melody, Melissa, Sandy, Sara, Sara, and Shana: Thank you for your friendship and willingness to add to this book. Your experiences and wisdom made it much better! I am so glad to share life with you.

To my parents, Dan and Karen: Thank you for loving us and working so hard for us. Thank you for taking us to church three times a week and making sure we made it to vacation Bible school, youth group, and church camp. Thank you for teaching me that honoring God doesn't require perfection. I love you so much!

To my in-laws, Larry and Cheryl: Thank you for raising such a wonderful son! He is a tremendous blessing to me, and you are too. Thank you for your love, prayers, babysitting, and encouragement.

To my children, Audrey and Caleb: I hope with every word of this book you feel my love for you. You're turning out to be the greatest kids, despite your crazy mother. Probably your father has a lot to do with your wonderfulness.

To my husband, Eric: Without your love and support there would have been no book. Thank you for your encouragement and quirky sense of humor. You are my best friend and I love sharing life with you.

To my Savior, Jesus Christ: All I have is yours; all I do is for you. May I live every day in thankfulness for your sacrifice at the cross.

Note to the Reader

The publisher invites you to share your response to the message of this book by writing Discovery House Publishers, P.O. Box 3566, Grand Rapids, MI 49501, U.S.A. For information about other Discovery House books, music, videos, or DVDs, contact us at the same address or call 1-800-653-8333. Find us on the Internet at www.dhp.org or send e-mail to books@dhp.org.

About the Author

Jessie Clemence was a parenting expert for the first trimester of her first pregnancy. When reality intruded and she lost confidence in her own expertise, she began to seek her heavenly Father's parenting wisdom and insight. She now parents, and writes, with God's direction and grace. She loves reading, decorating her house, and vacationing. Jessie and her husband have two children  and live in southwestern Michigan.

Jessie graduated from Western Michigan University with a degree in Family Studies and worked in the foster care system before her children were born. Her writing has appeared in the magazine *MaryJanesFarm* and in *Money Matters*, a publication of Crown Financial Ministries. You can keep up with recent life events at her blog, www.jessieclemence.com.